PENGUIN BOOKS

DRUNK MOM

Jowita Bydlowska was born in Warsaw, Poland, and moved to
Canada as a teenager. She lives in Toronto, Canada, with her son
and his father.

DRUNK MOM

A MEMOIR

JOWITA BYDLOWSKA

Penguin Books

PENGUIN BOOKS
Published by the Penguin Group
Penguin Group (USA) LLC
375 Hudson Street
New York, New York 10014

USA | Canada | UK | Ireland | Australia | New Zealand | India | South Africa | China
penguin.com
A Penguin Random House Company

First published in Canada by Doubleday Canada, a division of Random House of
Canada Limited 2013
Published in Penguin Books 2014

LIBRARY OF CONGRESS CATALOGING-IN-PUBLICATION DATA
Bydlowska, Jowita.
Drunk mom : a memoir / Jowita Bydlowska.
pages cm
ISBN 978-0-14-312650-8
1. Bydlowska, Jowita.   2. Alcoholics—Canada—Biography.
3. Mothers—Canada—Biography.   I. Title.
HV5307.B93 2014
362.292092—dc23
[B]
2013049368

Printed in the United States of America
1   3   5   7   9   10   8   6   4   2

Set in Van Dijck MT Std

Penguin is committed to publishing works of quality and integrity. In that spirit, we are proud to
offer this book to our readers; however, the story, the experiences, and the words are the author's
alone.

This is not "to" or "for" Misiu
but because I'm sorry, Misiu.

CONTENTS

DRUNK
MOM

A NIGHT AT THE MUSEUM

One evening I find a baggie of cocaine.

The cocaine is in the washroom in the big museum in the city. Not the place you'd expect, but that's where I find it. The powder sits perfectly, almost neon white, in its plastic baggie stamped with pictures of tiny marijuana leaves. It just sits there, on top of the toilet-paper container. Unbelievable.

So what do I do?

I pour the powder down the toilet.

No, no I don't. I fish the flat makeup-mirror compact out of my clutch and set it on top of the toilet-paper container. I pour the powder onto the shiny surface. I use the business card of the annoying man who hit on me in the elevator to cut a big fat line. A slug of a line. This is the first part.

———

It's been a long time since I've done this.

———

Above the mirror, I look deep into my nostrils, at the sudden double chin, my own upside-down eyes—you stupid, stupid shit—and I think about the baby, how horrible this is, what I'm about to do— you stupid, stupid shit. I also think how no one ever just finds a baggie of cocaine like this, how this is an opportunity of a sort, how I'm totally lying to myself right now, this is no opportunity, this is horrible and illegal and evil, and then I remember the second part.

I take out a $20 bill from my wallet. I roll it. I put it against my nostril. And off I go. I'm no longer woozy from booze.

———

I charge back into the museum's restaurant to the party I'm offi- cially attending. I wonder if people will be able to tell, but I don't care right now, I'm beautiful. I got my nails done specifically for this stupid party and they are red and shiny like blood. God, yes: my hands are narrow and gorgeous with their ruby tips.

A woman named something like Gigi stops me and says that I look fantastic.

Thanks.

How are things?

Great. Great.

How's the baby? Where is he tonight?

He's with my sister.

How sweet.

I take out my wallet. The cocaine is behind the bank card.

I turn the picture flap around. I turn the wallet so that Gigi can see it. The picture of the baby.

She says that he's adorable and then says something about her own baby but I interrupt her because I can't listen to this.

Listen, I say, I'm so sorry to do this.

She tilts her head. She says, Do what? What is it?

I just have to go right now, I explain, because I'm late. I have to hit another party.

She smiles, her waxy hand touching me on the shoulder. Oh, no worries, no worries.

No worries. What a nice thing to say. No worries.

I feel like she could be a friend. We could become great friends. We could have adventures together. Talk about our babies.

We should go out for a coffee sometime, she says. Catch up.

We should, I say.

And in this exact instant the desire to become friends with her leaves me. I imagine us sometime in this future, standing in line, our trays stacked with tiny plastic cups filled with weirdly shaped leaves, some kind of a baby lettuce mix, at a place that is shiny and white, some kind of a place where she goes, and where I don't go, and we are talking about some richer girlfriend she hates, and about bad sex with her husband, and about cracked nipples and sleep training, and I'm completely dead inside.

She air-kisses me on both sides of my face. Excellent, she says. I'll call you.

For sure. Call me. I air-kiss her quickly back, say, Thank you. We have to get together. To talk about babies.

She's already turned halfway to talk to a woman who looks just like her but is even more stretched-out around the eyes. She says, Lovely to see you—to her, or to me walking away.

———

There is no other party. But I can't stay here. I have to go somewhere.

I want something.

I want a cigarette. I really want a cigarette. I want two cigarettes. Four.

I'd like another drink too, but with the coke in me I can hold off. But I really need to smoke.

Maybe another line.

I want something.

This is no ordinary wanting.

This is the wanting that has no end.

It's an obscene appetite; it's uncontrollable with mouth wide open, insisting. It's a baby—a wet, hungry baby that no one is picking up to soothe.

But I'm not a baby, am I? No. And you'd think an intelligent person would stay away, walk away from this kind of wanting.

Yes, an intelligent person would walk away, knowing well that the next warm hit of a drink—or a puff of a cigarette, or the drip in the back of your throat from cocaine—is only pleasurable for a short time.

An intelligent person would remember that the soothing inner hug of the wanting being satisfied is brief. It is receding even as I acknowledge it. And it has to be repeated to reactivate the feeling of comfort. Until it reaches oblivion, blackout.

You'd think an intelligent person would remember all that when she is in the throes of wanting. But this intelligence is no match for the kinds of instincts that demand to be satisfied instantly. And there's fear behind the wanting—the fear that if the wanting gets denied there will be only pain and the fear itself left.

I mean, come on, who doesn't want to press the button to relax instantly? Achieve instant pleasure? Instant relief? Is there anything better than that?

Perhaps. I've heard of meditating. Sitting still. Biding your time. Hard work paying off. Yes.

There are meditators and sittingstillers and timebiders and hard workers. I know. I know. But right now I am very uncomfortable because I want more. I want more relief.

Perhaps I am always uncomfortable. But what is *always*? There's only right now. Have I not achieved what the wise always talk about: living in the moment? I have. And the moment is uncomfortable. Just this moment.

I could wait.

But what if I die five minutes from now?

See, my discomfort is here, right now, and this is the only reality that matters: here and right now. And here and right now I am wanting. Something. To fix it.

Give it to me.

I want this to stop. I want ease.

I'm exactly like a baby. Pounding his heels against the mattress when distressed. Give it to me. Give it to me right now. His face twitching, he cries; he hiccups from crying, he can't stop. He won't stop until there's comfort. Whether it's a breast or a dry diaper or being turned over onto his belly—it has to happen right now. Now. Now. There is no waiting, no biding time. The wanting is enormous; it swallows him whole in lung-emptying breaths.

I get it. I get the screaming baby.

Because my wanting is just as powerful.

———

I could run. Maybe if I run I'll get there faster. Of course I'll get there faster. Where? Everywhere.

I want everything. All of it.

But I know it won't be enough. I decide to walk it off. Whatever is left of my reason insists on walking.

Walk. Don't think. Don't think about the cocaine.

Actually, I hate cocaine. I hated it before and I hate it now. Even though it makes me happy. But also so unhappy. Yes, I'm completely unhappy and I want to do more to fix it. That doesn't make sense. But if I do a little more, I'll be better, I know.

It's always this way.

———

I wonder if I should call the man who hit on me in the elevator on my way to the party. I guessed he was in his forties, with a nice suit on, an expensive suit, a silk tie. He looked like the kind of man who wouldn't be worried about doing cocaine with a stranger. And he could probably get more. He looked like the kind of man who could get more cocaine. More of everything. There was a vibe about him, something like a halo of owning expensive things, like an I-don't-need-to-give-a-fuck halo, he was that sort of man. Moneybags man. He said he was in sales. He asked what I did.

I could've picked a few things. I could've lied. I can't remember why I told him that I was a new mom. I suppose I just tell people that all the time.

I can't remember why he annoyed me. Maybe how insistent he was with his stupid card, looking at my chest and belly as if he wasn't being challenged by the idea that a baby just came out of the woman he was imagining having sex with. Maybe this only made him want to have me more.

———

I don't call the man. I walk and smoke.

I love it. I love smoking. I want to smoke more.

Eventually I have to take a break, because I'm starting to have trouble breathing. I hate taking this break. All I have in my head the entire time is the red glowing tip, the swirling smoke, the white cylinder consumed by the red, turning gray, black.

After what seems like nothing and forever at the same time, the cocaine rollercoaster finally starts to slow down. I'm thinking about doing more but I'm good, I'm good.

I'm good now.

I walk all the way home from the museum. It's a long walk. I'm trying to walk away from *wanting*.

———

I wonder how long cocaine stays in breast milk.

———

At home, my sister is asleep on the pullout bed in the living room. Sleeping, she looks twelve, even though she's twice that age. She's my first baby. I want to kiss her on the forehead as if she were a baby. I blow her a kiss instead. I worry my cigarette-cocaine-booze smell will wake her up. She is pure. Nothing like me.

I turn the light on to see my way up the stairs, memorize them before I go. I turn the light off, climb the stairs, hold my breath.

I close my eyes. The afterlights turn into flower shapes under my eyelids. Flowers in my head. Flowerheads.

I open my eyes. Let them get used to the darkness. And then I see the top of his head, the little fist like a flower bud. He's only an infant, still closed to the world in his few-months-old form, so fragile with soft skull, neck that holds his perfect head away from me. Because, thankfully, he's turned away from me. I couldn't bear to see his face right now. I hear him breathe. His breathing so delicate, rose petals falling.

He is asleep in his crib. In the meadow of pillows and soft toys.

I think of kissing him on the forehead. The notion is so strong that my mouth waters.

I don't kiss him. I can't go near him right now. It's poison.

I'm poison.

It's torture to watch him and not touch.

There's nothing I want more in my life than to go near him.

No, that's a lie. There are other things that I want more—of—in my life.

———

I tiptoe back down the stairs, in the familiar darkness.

My lungs are expanding. There's a wave of clarity going through my head like an electric zap. I don't want it. I want the zap to go away, I want to stay unzapped, high.

But I can feel myself sobering up. I don't like it. Soon, I will be folded into a knees-to-chin ball of fear. My throat is tightening already. And my nose is rooting like a baby's mouth for more.

The house is asleep. Outside, the beginnings of a new day are in the making. It's still too early for birds but I swear I can already hear them fussing around in their fucking nests.

I can't face any of it yet.

I grab my wallet. I lock the bathroom door just in case.

THE NEXT DAY

The cocaine hangover is a bit of a surprise. It's dull. It's dullness all over my body and a stuffy nose. I forgot this part.

I blow my nose over and over for the good feeling that I'm getting rid of the stuff in it. I'm not. Cocaine is ingested into the bloodstream right away. There's nothing you can do to get rid of it.

How do I know this? Before bed, I Googled until 4 A.M. to read about cocaine and breast milk and found out that it stays in the system anywhere from twenty-four to seventy-two hours.

Seventy-two hours. Christ.

This morning I had to go out, all bleary, stuffed-up and tired, and buy more formula. I tried to recall what it was like to be twenty-five and full of energy after a night like this. I remember experiencing the world in two dimensions, as if depth washed out completely, leaving everything looking like a cardboard cut-out of itself. It is bizarre to me that I used to be able to do this night after night. That's what twenty-five was like.

———

I shake and open the can of premixed formula. I pour it into a bottle, heat it up under hot running water.

The baby falls back asleep after the first few gulps.

———

At the door, on her way out, my sister asks me how I am.

I say, fine.

Her eyes say, No you're not.

She says, Okay. Are you going to be okay?

What do you mean? I'm the big sister. You can't ask me that.

She says nothing.

I'm just kidding. Jesus.

Okay, she says. She doesn't say much more. She's being distant this morning.

What's up with you?

Nothing. I'll call you later.

———

After she leaves and after the second feeding, I decide to take a bath. I want to wash off the dusty dullness.

The bruises on my breasts are fading. They were dark, almost black in some places. After this prolonged break they're getting lighter. I have to be more diligent about this, I tell myself. Who knows what kinds of damage he's doing. Sometimes I get too tired to move his mouth back onto a nipple. Before the bath, I squeeze the nipples to relieve all the milk that's stretching and filling up under my skin, making my breasts rock-hard.

I watch the thin streams of pearly fluid shoot, explode against the sink. I feel sad, defeated. What a waste.

But I quickly snap out of this thought. It's not a waste. It's poison. It's all poison, poison going down the drain.

He starts to cry as soon as I lie down in the bathtub. He has the worst sense of timing. He cries as soon as I sit down to a meal, when I need to shit, do my makeup, have sex, when the doorbell rings, when I take baths. He stays silent and content when I surf the Net in boredom, does nothing when hours stretch into megahours.

I get out of the bathtub—my body feeling broken, mangled from the night before—and I stumble toward the laundry room which is a nursery, which is a laundry room, which is a nursery.

The open mouth is one big scream. The baby is a lung being robbed of air.

My breasts pulse painfully and gently in response, in their own instinctive scream.

I lift him up and he grabs for them. With his eyes shut, a wrinkled face with a horrible grimace on it, he looks like a frantic, blind old man. He's a frantic old man grabbing for young tits.

I gently move his hands and he twists his body as if in pain. I give him his bottle with formula. He sucks hungrily. His eyes remain closed.

My boyfriend is coming back later. He calls and says he can't wait to see his little family.

Little family, that's us.

———

But before my boyfriend gets home that evening I leave the house. Outside, still stuffed-up and cocaine-hungover but already shaky with anticipation, I pick up the pace and I start to sing. I sing to my baby in the stroller and I sing that we are doom-doom-doomed. But it's a happy song. Well, not that happy, but it's not like I can do anything about where I'm going right now—even though I know I should not go there—and I feel like singing because I'm excited. I'm excited about where I'm going.

Over the canopy of the stroller, I can see the top of the baby's blue too-small hat. A friend's mother made the hat but she has passed on, so I always think of death when I look at this blue hat.

Out of respect—for death? for my friend's dead mother?—I make the baby wear the hat all the time and don't dare exchange it for a bigger one. It has a shiny marble of a button so that the side flaps can sit tightly over the ears when you button it up under the chin. The flaps push his cheeks a little forward and with the blue pompom on top of the hat and those big, round pink cheeks, my infant looks ridiculous, like a caricature of a baby.

If nothing else, think of him in his blue hat, says my boyfriend later on, maybe even that evening when we talk about my drinking again. I understand what he's doing. He wants me to think of Frankie in the hat, looking cute and helpless, and he thinks that this will stop me, the image of him.

But nothing stops me these days.

I'M A DRUNK

Oh, in case you're wondering: I'm not a cocaine addict.

I prefer to drink.

You found me in the middle of my story and I happened to have just found a baggie of cocaine in that bathroom.

But honestly, I prefer drinking.

I prefer drinking to anything in the world: sex, food, sleep. My child, my lover, anything.

I love to drink. Sometimes I think: No, I *am* drink.

It's like my blood. Even before I get it, I can feel it in my veins. I'm not being poetic—I can actually feel it in my veins.

It's gold. It's like little zaps of gold going through me, charging me, starting me up.

When I drink, I fill with real gold and become god-like.

So I'm not a cocaine addict. I'm a drunk.

I had been a drunk for a long time. I stopped drinking for a time, and then I started again.

I believe that you're never cured of alcoholism. I use the word *cure* but it is not strictly a disease. Go to any AA meeting, watch or read anything about addiction, and sooner or later you will hear the word "disease." But it is not a disease. Disease implies you can maybe cure it. In my opinion it's closer to a condition or, perhaps, a habit you can't unlearn completely once you stop it. Even if dormant, it is ingrained in you.

For example, my first language is Polish. I don't use it often yet I will never unlearn it. When needed, I can speak it fluently, just like that.

I'm always going to be a speaker of the language of alcoholism too—if I relapse, picking up right where I left off, catching up to my last number of drinks with an extra drink to top it off, my vocabulary expanding.

People also tend to mistake alcoholism for drinking: "I'm going to slow down. Cut down on my drinking." Okay. You do that. But if you're an alcoholic, you can't do just that. Alcoholism is not drinking, just like hemophilia is not bleeding. You can't slow down, cut down on your alcoholism. You can't unlearn its language. You can stop using it and forget some of the words, but you still know it. With drinking too, you can stop drinking and hope it'll stay stopped. Alcoholism is a habit, a permanent condition of having the habit—like this *wanting* is, at least in my case. Sometimes the wanting gets too strong and I run. I run with it, run so fast I'm out of breath, and then run even faster.

I relapsed when the wanting got particularly strong.

To relapse means to "suffer deterioration after a period of improvement."

There was a period of improvement when I became sober for the first time, at the age of twenty-seven. But before that, I was the kind of drunk girl who ran so fast with it, drinking, she could never catch her breath.

I was the girl who danced barefoot on tables or sometimes fell asleep with her shoes on, or sometimes lost a job or a relationship. I was the type of tragic girl that boys would try to fix, or try to drink with although only until they'd had enough, and there I would be, moving apartments yet again only to move in with another boyfriend who claimed he'd be better at fixing me.

I always had three drinks to your one, I always prepared for a night out with a bottle of wine, always opened another beer at 4 A.M., after coming home after a night of partying.

But it's easy to hide your drinking in your twenties, when many of your peers seem to be bent on oblivion too, when comparing hangovers is par for the course. Except that I kept quiet when people discussed having blacked out as if it was something unusual. It happened to me all the time. And I too shook my head in disbelief when a friend would do something silly while intoxicated—steal a garden gnome, climb on a roof, make out with not-his-girlfriend. Look at that guy! Guy, you really need to cut down on your drinking!

Me? You couldn't catch me. I juggled friends and environments. Except for those poor boyfriends, there weren't that many people who witnessed my demise. It's easy to flit from party to party, from event to event when you're full of life in your twenties. It's easy to drink in your room before you go out to flit—the people you keep around you in your twenties are new to it all. They are new to friends drinking in their rooms or friends in Emergency because of alcohol poisoning. And they are flitters as well; we all flit, trying to catch up with each other and outflit each other too.

The ones who drink a little harder can even make fun of themselves with typical youthful bravado. I remember sitting with a heavy-drinking friend and joking that once we reached twenty-five, we'd definitely have to go to Alcoholics Anonymous because this was just ridiculous, how drunk we were getting all the time.

She stumbled home, and I opened a third bottle of wine and wrote about that in my journal, or tried to write. Mostly I just scribbled. *Go to AA when you 25 stupid bitch.*

I went to AA when I was twenty-seven. At that point, I had lost another relationship and a job that I'd gotten freshly out of grad school. My roommates were planning to kick me out. As they say in AA, "AA was the last house on the street." There were no other options.

I stayed in AA for three and a half years. I stayed sober.

But now I'm not.

I've relapsed.

I don't know why. Or I know why and I don't have the time to go over it right now. Or there are too many whys to consider. Or who really cares why?

The point is, I really, really need a drink.

———

When I walk into a liquor store—against my will, not because I want to, I promise, I swear—I know that I own my two feet but I don't, really; they're no longer mine. And as soon as I'm inside the store—with its golden colors and lights, like one big liquid carnival—I know that no power in this world can make me leave before I've gotten something.

Yes, there's a thought buried somewhere deep under a pile of much more urging, loud thoughts, that says I can leave, I don't have to do this . . . but this little thought is so weak, it will never overpower everything else that's going on inside me.

———

I don't blame you for hating me for not wanting to stop. For relapsing and not wanting to stop.

It happened because my best friend fell in love.

Or because I felt old.

Or it happened because I was far away from home.

It just happened.

Because I wanted a drink. Because the wanting was stronger than me.

It was at my best friend's bachelorette. It was vodka and soda. I don't know how it ended up in my hand. Or rather, I do know: the bartender asked me—as they always do—*Just* soda? and just like that I changed my mind.

No, *vodka* and soda, I said.

I drank it like it was just soda. I looked around. No one paid any attention. No one would anyway. People drink all the time.

I was downstairs. I was the non-drinker sent to get drinks for all the bachelorette women upstairs. The bar was red and velvet and gold. It was fall, my birth month, my birthplace. Warsaw. Another one, please, I said to the bartender then.

What did he know?

Double, actually.

I didn't get sloppy that night, no blackouts. But at one point that night, in another place, a high-end Malibu Barbie–infested club, I snatched someone's drink and drained the bottle in one practiced gulp. It was the gulp that was familiar. Too familiar.

In less than two hours I annihilated three and a half years of sobriety and caught up to right where I left off.

———

Two days later, my best friend's wedding started with a couple of shots of vodka and a bunch of Ativans. Kneeling in church behind her giant puffy dress, I felt laughter coming on, possibly caused by the theatricality of the ceremony, possibly by vodka and Ativan arm-wrestling in my brain. I managed to swallow my giggles, turn them into a cough. I coughed a lot through that very serious hour in church.

Outside afterwards, I had trouble pinning my best friend's veil to the back of her head as she received guests and flowers.

The wind was really strong that day.

———

The wedding ended with my waking up sick in an unfamiliar hotel room.

I woke up with flashbacks of burning my maid-of-honor dress with a cigarette, stuffing my face with cake and fish at the same time, flexing my muscles and laughing manically when pictures were taken, fending off my best friend's boy-cousins who tried to kiss me, dancing with my best friend's sister's husband and telling him that I'd wanted to sleep with him back in the day when he was much thinner. I remember telling him, too, that I had to do a pregnancy test the next day. I had been feeling funny lately.

And you're drinking?

If I'm preggers it's the last time I'll party so it's totally okay, I told him.

We danced.

Later, someone carried me through darkness, my body half leaning on his back.

This is all that I recalled the next day when I woke up in the unfamiliar room.

At home, I puked for hours. Then I slept.

In the evening I bought the pregnancy test, found out I was pregnant.

———

There's an expression in AA, "to white-knuckle," which means not drinking but not going to meetings either. It implies a struggle: clenching your fists so tightly as you're trying to hang on to your sobriety that your bones shine through your skin.

I don't believe that AA is the only way to stay sober, by the way. However, it was the only way I had managed to stay sober for a long time before I relapsed. And now I definitely wasn't going to AA meetings but I was definitely trying to stay sober while pregnant. It was a period of almost-grace. I white-knuckled some of the time, but for most of it, I was in such awe of my pregnancy and I was so scared of hurting the little boy growing inside my belly that I didn't struggle that often.

It worked with the exception of holidays, when I drank somberly and greedily, a glass of wine on Christmas Eve, three glasses on New Year's Eve, every drop like a hiss against a hot surface. My wanting burning bright.

MOTHERHOOD

Here's how it is: One day I wake up and it turns out that I am now the head of a country. A whole country—imagine that!

What happens is that I've been given a crown one very painful morning and now the entire country depends on me. Not only that, but because of my genetic makeup it is obvious to everyone around me that I'll naturally know how to rule this country: how to feed it and protect it from disasters and attacks. How to make its people happy. As the genetically designated and designed monarch, it is expected of me that I will know exactly what to do with the little people who depend on me, that my nature will dictate how to help them and feed them and clothe them.

To help me rule it properly, I've been given a gift: an endless supply of food that the country's people live on.

I'm also given a generous pension for ruling this country. Free money that comes every two weeks from the government. The king (there is a king!) insists I am given this money to do my job as the ruler. It is precisely why I've been given this money by the government. Me and not him. He is right.

Not only that—to prove myself as a worthy ruler, I've been given a whole year off from my other duties that usually involve sitting in a windowless office and typing on a computer. It's also strongly suggested I put my un-duties—such as writing novels and taking photographs—on hold. The things that take up time and bring no money and do absolutely nothing for the good of the country.

When I say "it's suggested" I don't remember if an actual person suggests this, if everyone perhaps suggests this or if it's just me going through the bouts of guilt. I do those wasteful things from time to time anyway, but the sense that they take away from the people of my country is overwhelming and creates anxiety. And guilt.

By the way, the first time the country goes through a serious internal conflict, it is over guilt about that money when it starts coming in. I quickly learn that the guilt is part of the responsibility that I've been given as the new ruler. It is unavoidable, like taxes.

There will be more guilt. So much guilt. Some of it will be so severe that the country will be undergoing constant economic sanctions. Eventually the country will have to declare bankruptcy. I will try to run the country while bankrupt for a while, which will only produce more sanctions, more guilt.

And there will be more trouble to come along, riots and disobedience so devastating that martial law will have to be imposed over my country—an intervention of military authorities due to an on-going emergency.

———

Finally, there will be shame.

It will be the shame that I am failing myself as a monarch—and how ungrateful of me when so many women want to rule countries and can't!—and that I am failing my loving king and the king's mother and my beautiful, supportive sister and my mother and my father and most of all the people of my country. The sweet little people who depend on me so much. Who cannot go to another country because I am theirs and they're mine and I've accepted the crown without any doubt in my heart that this was precisely what I wanted.

———

But right now we're in the beginning of my reign. After the crowning, the people are waiting outside my queenly tower and they are hungry, naked and somewhat angry.

The crown is a little tight on my head but I come out on the balcony and show them my breasts bursting with milk and they cheer in admiration and with voracious need, and I feel powerful and loved. I feel that I'm the right ruler of this place—there was no mistake that I've been chosen to do this.

Besides, if I've any doubt about my ability to handle the responsibility, I am told of millions of monarchs like me who have handled their little queendoms just fine. People in my own family can testify—and readily do—how ruling a country comes naturally for my gender. There's no magic to it. Sure, there will be mistakes, but it's expected that my natural instincts will overrule selfishness, helplessness, fear . . . alcoholism. My strong will to do well as a ruler will be enough to protect me from the darkness that's engulfing my heart.

The natural instincts will ensure that I will not poison the food source for the people who depend on me. That I will not let it out into the sea (the sink) and give my people artificially manufactured substitute. That I will not endanger my people in any way—even if it's just because of the egomaniacal prohibition: the fact that they are flesh of my flesh, blood of my blood.

But mostly because of the deep, instant, desperate love I have for my people. After all, I love my country. I would die for my country.

After all, I knew that I would be a ruler of it one day, that the people would depend on me. That it would be expected of me to handle this responsibility. That I would know exactly what to do because we, women, just do. My mother-in-law just knew what to do and my own mother supposedly knew exactly what to do. And even my grandmother knew what to do even though she had been secretly shipped away to a sanatorium for two years, after giving birth to her own country, for something known as "melancholic nature." They didn't have the term "postpartum depression" back then. And as one of the women in my family once actually said, they didn't have the luxury of calling nonsense a psychological disorder.

———

I don't know if what I'm going through as a new mother is postpartum depression. It is suggested to me more than once, and I use the term to excuse why I'm failing so much in my new role. But even that comes with guilt. Why can't I just snap out of it? I'm even taking medication—Prozac—to help me deal with depression, but it doesn't seem to help because I keep deteriorating anyway and post-partum depression sounds like a luxurious term to me too, a luxurious excuse to cover what I deeply believe to be a moral failing.

———

When I found out I was pregnant I knew right away that I wanted to have this child. I didn't tell my boyfriend for a while because the child wasn't planned, and I felt guilt over that as well. I had the guilt over trapping him—I didn't plan to trap him, but my body had other plans.

My boyfriend was a fulfilled man, a successful man, a man who was quite vocal about not wanting children, a man who enjoyed going out with his friends and having a fabulous life of semi-bachelordom.

When I finally told him about the pregnancy (middle of the night, my eyes suddenly springing open out of fear, words spilling out: If you don't want it, I'll be fine on my own), he was happy and scared. Mostly happy.

I was grateful and overwhelmed that he wanted to have a family with me. Me with my imperfections, my depressions, and even me with my then-dormant addiction hanging over us like an ever-present shadow.

I found his love and joy generous and I told myself to not screw it up.

I wanted to be what he wanted me to be—a good mom, a worthy partner, a perfect ruler for the country that he had accidentally given me.

And every time I'd fail (the baby, him, me, our royal family), I'd feel remorse so great that it weighed me down like a crown made out of lead. The remorse crushed any expectations that he or I had had about my ability to rule properly.

———

Metaphors aside, all he wanted and all I wanted for me was to just be normal, to just be a healthy, fulfilled woman who cares for her child. All I had to do was be a mother to a little baby. That is all. Just a mother.

Easing into the expectation.

Easing into motherhood.

BEDTIME

I t is now July, a month after my son was born. I'm having drinks with a new friend who wants to help me out with my artistic project.

Nice guy.

I used to be an alcoholic, I tell him, when I order another round for us, but I'm not now. This is my day off, that's all. I never get days off now. The baby. It's a lot of work, as they say.

It is, he agrees.

But I don't really drink, I say. Not anymore—much. Not much at all. I drink just like anybody else. Not much at all.

He nods, Sure.

Because it's not *that much*. It's not that big of a deal, really. Can I even call this a relapse? A drinking problem? Please. Do I sit behind a dumpster with a paper bag? No. I do not sit with a paper bag behind a dumpster. Do I fall down, break legs? No, I do not fall down.

I don't fall asleep on park benches, don't leave the stroller in stores with Frankie forgotten in it. I don't shout and throw purses at my boyfriend in a drunken rage. I'm nice. I wash. I wash Frankie. I don't forget about his formula if I have a little too much. But I almost never do have a little too much.

But if I have a little too much, I'm responsible. I drink after he goes to sleep. I don't forget to check on him before I do. I check on my boyfriend asleep. Don't forget to fold our family's laundry. I manage. Everything is manageable. And it's not really a relapse; it's nothing. It's just like anybody else.

When Frankie was born I was completely sober. I drank alcohol twice when I was pregnant but it was nothing, nothing that took a hold of me; I was responsible. And anyway, I felt too sick to drink.

Frankie was born to a sober mother.

And after Frankie was born some friends came over. There was champagne. We celebrated. Just like anybody else would.

Then there was another big party, to welcome Frankie to the world. So many nice, friendly people showed up. They brought presents, stiff paper bags filled with bottles too. We took the bottles out of the bags, naturally. As they appreciated the newborn, we read the labels on the bottles while holding them by their necks, tilting them in another kind of appreciation.

They drank. I drank, they drank, we drank, Frankie slept in his bassinet.

And after that, there were still people coming by with presents, a procession of people, Scotch for my boyfriend, wooden ecological toys for Frankie; this was after all the parties. Sometimes it was just one person, one bottle. It was nothing. It was celebrating.

So I've been drinking a little since my friend's wedding, god, no, not that much, technically, practically nothing, a sip here and there in the stream of celebratory sips. And now, not much at all. Every other day, if that, but it's mostly wine, it's civilized. I drink it with my meals. I try to learn about wine. You can pair one wine with fish, another with red meat.

I don't say any of this to my friend. But just in case I say, Yeah, I've got it under control.

I know you do, he says like I'm not even there.

I say, Another one?

Sure.

My friend matches me drink for drink. He is at least twice my size.

We talk about babies.

Or I talk.

The C-section scar is still raised and red and crazy-looking. Really something. He doesn't want to see it. That is fine with me.

Things are starting to spin slightly.

I tell an anecdote about baby's projectile poop and my friend laughs. There are a few more rounds of drinks, the dinner crowd is starting to arrive. He asks me about the art project. We'll get to it, I promise.

I talk more about babies but at one point he cuts me off and says he has to pick up his own kid from soccer practice. He asks me if I'm going to be okay going home in this state.

I'm fine.

I get back on my bike. I make one stopover on my way home. This liquor store is close to home and I try not to come here too often. The drunken teenage buskers and behind-the-dumpster types are shockingly observant. You'd think they would be out of it, but no. Some of them have started saying hello when they see me, so lately I try to avoid this store. But today I risk it and stop by to pick up something extra for later on.

———

I didn't have a drink, you're pissing me off with these accusations, I say to my boyfriend when I get home.

He sniffs me again.

Please.

How was your meeting, he wants to know.

It was fine. We talked about art.

Your project?

What else.

Are you sure you're going to be okay if I leave?

Of course. I'll be fine. You're being really weird.

I'm sorry, he says.

———

When he gets back, I'm unconscious on the floor. He relates the whole story to me later, through clenched teeth.

The baby is in his wicker basket. The baby is screaming, possibly trying to outdo the bombastic sounds coming out of the speakers. All the lights are on. The boyfriend notices I've changed my dress while he's been out. I notice this too, on waking the next day.

The story continues.

First, he turns off the music.

He talks to me. Tries to talk to me. My ear against the carpet.

He suggests I get up.

I do nothing.

He orders me to get up.

Nothing.

Eventually, he has to give up and lifts my head and slaps me, hard, across the face. He tells me this, his eyes not wavering, not leaving my face as he says it: I had to slap you.

So he slaps me.

Nothing.

He pulls me up to my feet and lets me drop. He drags me to the bathroom and splashes my face with cold water. He shouts.

Nothing.

I am eventually dragged to bed, upstairs, deposited there with my clothes on. The door is closed.

———

Downstairs, in the wicker basket the baby is soaked in piss and milk and not calming down.

After my boyfriend rocks him for a while, the baby finally falls asleep. His face remains too pink hours later, irritated by all the accumulated snot and tears. He is barely 12 pounds, and his arms and legs remain curled up—they are still formed to fit in a womb. His eyes can't focus yet; there are still soft spots on his skull.

My boyfriend sits in his office chair with the sleeping baby in his arms, watching him breathe. My boyfriend doesn't sleep all night. He watches him breathe, all night. He didn't care if I was okay, he tells me. He was just watching the baby. Breathe.

There is no reason to hate me or to panic, I say when I get up the next morning in my different dress. This isn't going to happen again. I'm so stressed about the art project. I drank to calm my nerves. It backfired. But I'm not going to do that crazy thing again. Drink so much. I'm not going to drink at all, actually. I shouldn't anyway.

My boyfriend is silent.

Please.

Okay.

I love you guys, I say, and kiss the baby's head over and over. The smell of his head is milk, honey and sweet almonds, tears and spit. The combination—it's intoxicating.

I would never do anything to hurt you.

Okay, my boyfriend says again.

I really do love you. So much. This is the last time, I promise.

Okay.

Believe me?

What choice do I have? my boyfriend says.

BIRTHDAY

In August, on my boyfriend's birthday, we go out to one of those hipstery tapas restaurants. We order something small and potent. It comes to us on a square plate surrounded by thin paisleys of sauce.

It seems half a dozen of these places, these hip restaurants, pop up every week on the newly trendy street. The very cool ones have no names or keep the old convenience-store signs—*Family Fruit and Smokes*—or other former-business announcements such as *We Fix Pants*. The less cool ones with no old signs left over go for nonsense monikers, something that those delighting in irony would find particularly chuckle-worthy.

The place we're at is called something like Doodle Noodle. It's all orange decor on black walls; waitresses who seem barely four-teen totter around balancing tiny trays of tiny food.

The baby is at home with my sister.

By the time my boyfriend and I left for the evening, I had al-ready prepared by taking a long bath while enjoying four and a half big glasses of wine.

I was stressed about going out and not drinking. So I had a cou-ple of drinks. Problem solved.

Before another serving of wet bunny turds, I go into the bath-room at Doodle Noodle and dip into my purse. I always have some vodka on me these days. I cut into the lining of my purse and I keep the mickey there. I can finish a mickey, easy, in three goes by now.

Upstairs, after the mickey, we eat the bunny turds and talk. I don't know what we talk about. All I'm thinking about is the few fluid ounces of clear liquid sloshing back and forth in my head.

Gotta pee again, I announce, making sure I sound annoyed with myself.

I wear a good-girl dress, below the knees—lots of room to bal-ance well. I balance well. My heels are a good four inches high. The stairway is long and narrow. Lots of orange on the walls. It's like tightrope walking. I don't fall down.

The next thing I remember is sitting at the table upstairs again eating something oily and black. Maybe rapini. Maybe not.

In my head, there is relief and panic. Relief for the empty mickey stashed discreetly in the garbage pail downstairs—evidence gone, puff—panic because there is no more.

Pay attention.

He's asking me something, the boyfriend. There's more orange behind the shiny-haired waitress who is now at our table and says something that sounds like wah-wah-wah. It makes me giggle for some reason.

———

I negotiate a glass of wine. My boyfriend doesn't like me drinking but this is a special occasion. But I don't drink. Not ever! I explain this to him. I promise to drink slowly.

———

I drink slowly. I have to make it last. The waitress is asking us something again. I want to tell her to get lost but I remember not to.

———

More miniature food comes, or doesn't, perhaps it's just the bill; it is hard to tell with all this darkness and blur and tiny trays.

Next, I'm smooshing my boyfriend's face close to mine to take a picture of us with my cellphone. I smile very wide. As it turns out later, his face never makes it into the frame.

We're outside at this point. I have a great idea.

———

Thanks to my great idea, next, we're in a strip club. There are rows of chairs, mirrors, hair extensions, taut skin and fluorescent everything: signs, mesh. Neon. Of course, neon.

A flashback of me on the slick couch upstairs waiting. My boyfriend disappearing or coming back—no, no, disappearing—with my look-alike.

Wake up, a voice says.

The fat face of a bouncer in my face.

I'm awake.

Stairs to the bathroom.

In the bathroom, girls, glitter and fake eyelashes. A caterpillar of lashes falls into a sink.

Inside the stall, nothing behind the lining in my purse. How come? Where is it?

Back on the slick couch. My boyfriend says I have to go outside. We're going outside. We're going. Now.

Then the night. Nothing.

———

In the morning, silence, the whiteness of our bed and sun through the windows, merciless.

I can't remember much more than these sorts of bleeps.

Listen—

Yes, he says. His voice is too awake.

How long have you been up?

A while.

I apologize for ruining his birthday.

It's okay. I shouldn't have let you have that glass of wine.

I think about how he sounds as though he truly believes that's what did it. But I don't want to question his honesty, especially since I'm so caught up with lying myself.

———

I puke a little in the bathroom. I clean up. Come out, give him his birthday presents.

———

Later on we walk by the lake and take lots of pictures.

I'm wearing white and my hair is up in a loose bun. The baby is so tiny; he fits into the sturdy piece of cloth fastened into a sling that I wear over my right shoulder.

In the pictures I look angelic, kissing the top of the baby's head, posing with my sunglasses perched coyly on my head. There are a few pictures of my boyfriend too, and he looks older than he normally looks, maybe he even looks his age, despite the youthful outfit he's wearing and all the summer light that's so deceptive, making everything seem so carefree and innocent.

SUMMER

Since the baby, I'm out of the house a lot. I walk aimlessly for hours.

Outside, I think about my art project and I think about my baby. I am happy that I had him. The impossibility and possibility of him—it is mind-blowing.

I'm not a crier. Seriously. Although when I first saw Frankie a valve opened inside me and I was flooded with emotion so large that all I could do was cry, to try to flush it out, but the more I cried, the harder I cried and I couldn't stop.

On the operating table, twenty-three hours into labor, I saw the reflection in the surgeon's glasses of what was going on with my body. I saw what violation it took to get this child out, but it didn't matter. All I could think about was this tiny boy and how happy he had made me already.

I didn't know it at the time but it was too much happiness. Happiness puts you at too much risk—what if you were to lose it? Too much happiness is a paradox. It's a tragedy, even: getting something you've always wanted but being unable to keep it.

This thing, this happiness, it was falling out of me, it was uncontainable, excessive, spilling along with my tears. My guts under the scalpel.

———

Walking around with the stroller, this is what I think about a lot: Frankie's birth. As an animal I've fulfilled my function. You'd think I'd get bored with thinking about it but I don't. When I saw him for the first time, it felt as if something detonated in my head, a big bang: hello, this is a new universe.

I was his mother from the first ultrasound. There was the windowless waiting room of orange plastic chairs and old magazines as I waited to be seen by the robotic technician who smeared my stomach with clear goo and laconically recited: there's the baby, this is the heart, do you want to listen to the heartbeat.

On the grainy screen of the ultrasound, thousands of dots and zigzags came together, tightened, then expanded, almost falling apart at the edges.

She said "the baby." And it was.

Afterwards in the bathroom, I tried to cry but I couldn't. The emotion was fetal—there but not fully formed. It hurt and soothed at the same time.

———

As I walk, I pass other mothers—women like me or not like me at all, their hands tied to the handles of their Bugaboos and

Stokkes. Aren't we a strange bunch, I think: adult women completely unplugged from our regular lives (our grown-up lunches and conference meetings and business trips and bachelorette martini parties and the gym) in order to attend to these helpless, alien creatures?

I suspect many of us aren't as shell-shocked as I seem to be, but occasionally I catch someone's eye and it's like meeting in the trenches: What the hell are we doing here? I have no idea. But I love it.

In my ongoing confusion over motherhood, I go back to replaying the moment when my son was finally out, to remind myself of that overwhelming happiness, to remind myself what I'm doing here. And I feel comforted, reassured even, and I flash back a smile to the next mother who passes, the look of recognition on her face.

I tell myself: It's going to be okay. I'm a mom. This is my mission. There's nothing strange going on here.

But even early in the day, there is already another ongoing thought cycle running alongside this one. I pretend it's not there.

It's thirsty.

———

When my boyfriend offers to take care of the baby in the evenings, I go out to ride my bike. I do this a couple of times that August. I ride my bike to the liquor store first. I get a six-pack of light, lime-flavored beer. The beer cans start to sweat as soon as I get them outside. It's been impossibly fantastically tropical today. Patio weather.

And the drinks? They're not really drinks.

It's not even like drinking, drinking this stuff. It's summer. It's because it's summer. Everyone drinks in the summer.

———

I pedal as fast as I can to the park by the lake. I find a bench far from the bike trail. The cans look like Sprite cans—the tint of green is close enough; there's the same illusion of freshness contained in the lemony graphic. It's perfect. I'm just a bike rider taking a break by the lake, having my pop.

The water is lovely, a nice dark blue peppered with clean, white boats. The park is full of runners and rollerbladers, moms with strollers. The sun is still out and I'm wearing a T-shirt even though it's past nine.

———

I drink two cans fast.

On the third, I feel my body click and tingle, the warmth spreading from my chest, down my belly, straight into my cunt and then farther down to my feet.

It's a total jolt of joy. Despite the jolt I seem to be made out of caramel. Or toffee. Or whatever makes me feel so sweet and so relaxed that I could melt.

I just love everything. I love everything. I love everybody.

I need to tell someone.

I can't call my house because I'm supposed to be riding my bike.

———

I call my father.

I never call my family. I don't know why. They're sweet people. No, they're not.

They are loving and funny, hateful and completely humorless.

They believe that Jesus Christ is our savior, but I remember them making fun of religious freaks when I was a little girl and they were atheists. They are intolerant of non-Europeans. But sometimes they are stunned by the small-mindedness of their Polish community here in Canada, people who they say judge too much.

I don't call them because I'm never sure that I won't hang up. In that way, I'm a product of my parents. I'm a product of two people who refuse to be defined and whose most powerful weapon is surprise and the predictability of being surprising.

My sister: "You know what mom's like."

Me: "Yeah. She freaked out, right?"

My sister: "She was totally calm. We had a really nice chat."

I don't talk to my parents because there's only so much unpredictability that I can handle, having myself to deal with. I cannot rely on my own two feet to walk me out of liquor stores—the disconnect between my mind and the ground I'm stepping on seems too great.

But when I'm buzzed, like right now, I don't worry about who's going to answer: which dual mom or dad. It doesn't really matter at all. I'm generous and feel infinitely tolerant when I'm drunk.

———

I smoke and drink another two cans as I talk to my father about the baby.

My father listens. Tries to say something but I'm talking now. I know I'm talking too much, Dad, but I just wanted to explain how I'm so full of happiness and everything is working out, isn't it? And I'm just calling to share my happiness.

He says—

Please, let me finish.

I drink my last can.

I talk more. And talk. Suddenly I share secrets with him, tell him that I never planned to be a mother but now that I am, I can't think of a more wonderful experience.

I tell him that I actually feel fulfilled for the first time in my life. And that I also feel a little cheated since I always thought myself to be above such basic biological determinants. I guess I always thought I'd be some kind of an academic or an artist and derive my satisfaction from that, I say to my dad. But like you—I boldly refer to a touchy topic: his abandoning his own writing aspirations—I think I can be quite content just being a parent. Perhaps I'll write later when the kid is older, right? I say, and my dad grunts something on the other end, something that I take as encouragement to talk more because I keep going.

I've never said any of this to anyone, I tell him. I tell him that I'm glad we have this kind of relationship, where we can just talk. I say that they're really confusing sometimes, he is, not just him but Mom too. The whole family. But I love them no matter what. I love him. I love my baby. Because now there's a new family member! Family is very important. Perhaps it's the only thing that matters, I mull. Family. It's great.

———

He starts to speak—

Oops, what time is it? I say.

I'm done with my can.

Once the last drop makes it out, I hang up.

I get back on my bike. I pedal home. I'm slightly buzzed but not buzzed enough to sing out loud. So I sing in my head, letting the end fragments of songs spill out of me once in a while as I keep going.

———

At home, my boyfriend says he's forgiven me for the night before.

What night before.

We kiss.

I hope the lemon smells strong enough to overpower the other, beery smell.

He holds me even closer.

Who cares what night before. I'm not going to ask.

———

When we make love I hold on to him with all my strength—I'm full of gratitude for his forgiveness. This gratitude is genuine.

I'm full of gratitude because I got away with whatever he has forgiven me for. I love him so much. I'm so happy.

I'm so happy because I remember something. Although it's not like I really forgot about it. I remember something that is waiting for me after we finish.

He holds my head and says that I don't seem to be entirely there, what's distracting me?

No, nothing, I assure him. I pull him even farther into myself.

I can't come but the evening isn't entirely lost yet.

I tune in to his body reaching farther inside mine, try to estimate how far from coming he is. I hold on to his ass. There's a tension of muscles underneath the palms of my hands. Close. Closer.

I say, Come on, come. Come for me.

The tension gets even stronger.

Come on.

There's still an almost full mickey hidden in a box in the basement.

HARM REDUCTION

There are lots of evenings when I go out on my bike with my pack of six beers. It's never just six beers either. The amounts, they increase. They have to as my body gets used to alcohol and it makes more space for it. It makes more space for it because it doesn't just want more of it—it needs more.

A need implies that this, my drinking, is something that is necessary.

Is it not necessary. Yet it is a need.

What kind of a need is it, then?

It's not a physical one. At least not yet. My lacking this thing is not going to result in death, not even a serious withdrawal, probably no alcoholic seizure.

This is a need that's psychological—sustenance necessary to keep troubling thoughts away. The thoughts of guilt and worry.

I can't imagine dealing with my guilt and worry without the anaesthetic of alcohol—the guilt and worry that haunt me when I'm conscious and aware. Sober.

Maybe another day, I can deal with it. Maybe tomorrow I can deal with it. Maybe after the weekend. Right now I just need a break.

It is ingrained in me now that once I take a drink, I will get the break, will get the relief. Yes, I know—intellectually—that the relief is brief and that the consequences can be awful, but I no longer have any defenses. I'm looking for the perfect out from my situation, and even though I know sobriety is the perfect out, it seems like an absurd concept. Can't get sober till I feel I'm ready to face the guilt and worry; can't face the guilt and worry when I'm sober.

I have to wonder, too, if in seeking this ultimate break I'm trying to subconsciously annihilate myself—if this is some manifestation of *Todestrieb*, a death wish. I wonder if my addiction is a strongly expressed death wish, nothing more, nothing less.

I don't consciously think of dying when I'm drinking. In fact, the desire that I imagine drives my drinking is the desire to live, to live loudly and freely, without any care. I want to jump, want to run, want to want!

But then there's the parallel, perhaps less conscious desire, which is to numb myself to the world. To deal with the world tomorrow.

Living is difficult. Dying is difficult. Being dead is not difficult. And what else is a blackout if not death?

———

Because of blackouts there are entire days when I try to avoid my boyfriend out of fear that he'll ask me about something from the night before.

The truth is, I don't remember the night before. Most of the time I remember only how I got there; there's some kind of a beginning—me drinking on the metal staircase outside—and then there's nothing for a long time, and then I'm in bed, waking up.

Sometimes there are painful, tender places on my body that I feel right away on waking, clues under the disguise of bruises. But I don't get to know the whole story despite the clues. The best I have are some guesses, like, I must've tried to prevent some serious fall judging by the way my shoulder feels.

———

We make love often, my boyfriend and I, because I want to distract him, to stop him from talking. We usually make love in the morning, but possibly not just in the morning because sometimes he'll say something or do something—like he'll tug on my hair—that will also seem to be a clue as to what happened the night before. Maybe something intimate, sweet, or something very, very filthy, but I wouldn't know.

Despite my avoiding him, my boyfriend is starting to ask questions too. The lovemaking is not enough to distract him. He asks about the tender, bruised places on my body, the way I smell, why I was so out of it—again—the night before when we had some friends over. Why I smoked an entire pack of cigarettes.

I think I know he knows and he probably knows I think I know he knows. But we still haven't really talked about it—about the fact that my drinking is starting to get out of control.

I'm not that bad. I need help. There's nothing wrong.

The doublethink is exhausting enough for me, I'm sure it's taking its toll on my boyfriend as well. But we never talk about it.

There are times too when I suspect my boyfriend wants to talk about it. But instead he is not talking to me at all, and that scares me too because I need him on my side—he's all I've got on my side.

At the same time, I'm grateful for his silence—it asks no questions and therefore there are no answers to give. So I don't ask him why he's quiet. I don't want him to answer. I don't think he wants to answer. We both pretend his silences are a new part of his personality.

The new parts of my personality are when I no longer mind that he still goes out a lot.

Since he's a new parent just like me, his sleep gets dramatically cut down and he doesn't go out as much as before, but he's still happily flitting from bar to bar at least a few times a month.

He's always been a social person—drinking Scotch with his men friends in private clubs, bar-hopping, flirting with PR girls, speaking at media events, playing poker till dawn. He's even picked up a new hobby—DJing—and came home once at 5 A.M., explaining that Mildred insisted he drop by for a nightcap afterwards.

I'm cross-eyed from a jaw-grindingly sober, sleepless night when he stumbles home that morning, but I say nothing because I'm already plotting how I'm going to get over this disappointment by drinking.

He tells me about his escapades because I ask. I joke that I'm living vicariously through him. I'm sure he doesn't tell me everything.

Which is okay because I don't tell him everything. I don't tell him anything.

Because of my drinking I consciously avoid conflict and confrontation. I no longer ask about his coffees with women who "needed help getting into the magazine industry."

In the past, this sort of eagerness (to help) often created tensions in our relationship, but now that I've secrets of my own, I've become generous and permissive, often even encouraging his socializing: What is Liz up to these days? Yes, I really do feel bad about Mildred's ex-husband being a dick, I think you should call her back.

———

Instead of focusing on my boyfriend's intriguing, socially devouring life, I should probably pay closer attention to mine. Life, that is—my simple, socially isolated life.

I need to sort myself out. Before I screw things up with the boyfriend or hurt myself badly enough to go beyond the bruises.

It is almost the end of August and I have had a continuous string of hollow nights and there may be clues everywhere, like puzzle pieces, but I can't put them together into anything coherent because there are too many blanks in between. The blanks trump whatever narrative I try to come up with.

This is because I'm a blackout drinker, *almost* always have been, and now that the blackouts are here—they are *always* here now—I start to feel a little concerned. As it was in the past, I am amused and worried about the person that takes over when I check out. She looks like me except that her eyes are gone. Replaced by marbles. Her legs are mine but the knees are inside-out. Her fingers dial numbers that I no longer remember; her mouth talks about things I have never even thought about or have tried not to think about. And what if perhaps she doesn't like children? Who's going to stop her?

I get scared enough to look up online some programs that deal with problems like mine.

Because I don't think I'm that bad (for example, you'd never see me hiding with a bottle of vodka in my bed at two in the afternoon, now, would you?), I decide I need a mild kind of solution. Not actual rehab but maybe rehab light. Despite being aware of the distance between wanting and needing getting smaller, I still harbor the idea that I haven't crossed the line. What kind of line I'm not entirely sure—perhaps the line that will divide the necessity from the absolute desperation.

I can't go all the way to admitting that my drinking is a big problem. Having gone to AA meetings in the past, I know I'm not capable of that kind of commitment. Right now, I don't even meet the only requirement of AA membership: a desire to stop drinking.

At this point, I still doublethink myself into agreeing that I only need a little adjustment to get back to feeling normal.

I don't know if I really need a program that deals with addictions—I wouldn't go that far—but at the same time, just in case, I know that I could do something to learn to manage better, to perhaps train my body to only want a bit—a can of lemon-tinted beer or two, no more—and to not disappoint me with another blackout.

So I'm looking for a commitment I can adhere to once a week tops, something I can explain—to myself, mostly—as a social thing, a thing I do to get away from the baby. Sort of like an activity that a girlfriend would tell me to partake in, a yoga class or ballroom dancing, to get me away from the baby. Some kind of *me*-time.

I find something that takes place once a week. It's called the

Guidance Self-Change Program, and it's to do with "harm reduction" and the negative consequences of drug use. Self-change reads to me like improvement. Improvement is always good. This is exactly like something a person interested in *me*-time could do: improve the person.

The program is offered at the local mental hospital, the Centre for Addiction and Mental Health. I remember laughing over that name with friends back in journalism school: you can get the addiction or you can get the mental health. I joke to myself now that I already have one—the addiction—but I need the other one. Badly.

I think, too, how much I like the phrase "harm reduction"—it almost sounds as if this thing was supposed to teach us how to drink. Like a course.

Or not drink. I'm not entirely sure I understand, but it's a short-term deal and that's all I need anyway, something short-term.

Because I need to learn how to drink properly. Or not drink.

———

You get into the program after doing a computer test at the hospital, which asks you: Do you crave a drink at a definite time daily? Have you ever missed a day of work because of your drinking? Do your loved ones remark on the way and/or the amount you drink? Things like that.

I have no idea if the questionnaire is set up so that it can detect you lying. But what would be the point? I answer as truthfully as I can.

After completing the questionnaire I find out that I have a problem. You only need to answer yes once to have a problem. Which is why everyone else taking the questionnaire today finds out the same thing—we all have a problem, no matter how many yeses.

All the people who passed the test—all of us who took it that day—get invited to the information session. Some guy says he said no to everything. The information-session lady says that just taking the questionnaire means you have a problem.

Of course it does.

We're all eligible for the harm-reduction.

Congratulations—I suppose.

I'm given a pamphlet about the program and a form to fill out.

———

There are two ways to reduce harm and tackle the program. The first is through eradicating drinking entirely, in other words, abstinence. The second is by drinking only a maximum number of drinks at a given time. So, for example, a maximum of three drinks on one occasion and a total of ten drinks a week. You can set any goal amount. If you go over that amount, you haven't met your goal.

In the Comments space on the form I'm tempted to make a lame joke about people setting their amount higher than what they'd normally drink. But I'm sure I wouldn't be the first to say it. I leave the Comments space blank.

———

During the program, the group is supposed to meet once a week and do homework in between.

I'm not entirely sure what happens once you graduate, but I hope I will be cured of my problem drinking.

If you don't meet your goal you are given some other alternatives, I'm told, one of which is meeting with the counselor one-on-one. You can also go to an inpatient facility, a rehab, if you're really struggling, but that, you're assured, is an option for you to explore after everything else fails.

This sounds like a threat to me, getting sent off to an inpatient facility, and I make myself a promise, which I have no way of securing. I tell myself—full of doubt already, somewhere behind all my doublethink—that I will never get that bad.

I think of the inpatient facilities I know from stories of people in AA, or from the television shows about addicts—especially the shows about addicts. My head is full of camera shots of young women with big terrified eyes, rimmed with pink from too much crying. The camera zooming in on their faces as they're getting whisked away to the place that will hopefully fix them but will most likely fail because forced confinement doesn't work for those who are in the throes of wanting: wanting to get out and just *wanting*—the wanting with no end.

The promise that I cannot secure but that I make regardless once I sign up for harm reduction is that I will never be the girl with hair whipping in my face as I stare wistfully out of the window of a car taking me to rehab.

ON THE BEACH

Before my *me*-time program starts, my boyfriend and I go on holiday by the ocean. We are staying at a cottage rental that we've found online. The baby is coming with us, of course.

I sing to the baby as we take off on the plane. I'm a little shaky on the plane. I don't like flying. Plus, I haven't had a drink in almost twenty-four hours.

The baby sleeps through the flight.

I bring a couple of mickeys with me. They are hidden at the bottom of the suitcase, behind the lining that you can open with a zipper. Suitcases were designed for liars.

———

I have to drink straight out of the bottle because our cottage is just one room, kitchen and dining room together, so there's a chance of getting caught if I were to mix. That's fine with me. More efficient this way.

If my boyfriend is inside the cottage, I have to sneak quick, brutally large gulps of pure vodka in the bathroom. I brush my teeth afterwards and put on extra deodorant so that the smells will block each other.

When the boyfriend is outside or napping, I drink with my head in the suitcase, right there behind our bed.

———

During the day we drive out to different beaches with the big wicker basket with the baby inside it. We are on the east coast of the East Coast and it's different here than anywhere else I've been to before where there are beaches. Here, the beaches are wild, huge, with people barely scattered on them. Unlike the more populated and sunny beaches of the west side, here the weather is capricious and cool so the beach culture is minimal, no loud frat guys with coolers full of beers, never any bikini-model girls. There is lots of fog. If you see people, usually it's just an elderly, spry couple walking hand-in-hand looking like an ad for a retirement home, or a few local families: sluggish children and their tired moms smoking, not swimming or walking. My boyfriend and I joke—in our big-city snobbishness—that they're just waiting till it's time to go home and eat their lunch hot dogs.

Sometimes there are local teenage surfers, usually boys, who come out even in sweater-and-raincoat weather and throw themselves right in the middle of the black suicidal waves that are frightening to even look at.

There are some beaches on the east coast where there are no people at all, and a few times we catch ourselves driving by various patches of sand looking for the most populated ones—sometimes we miss having people around. But most of the time we don't crave company at all, and we are happy setting up our small camp in the pale desert, with the wicker basket on the pure white sand, the ocean open and dark before us and a cold breeze always there under all the sun.

The baby naps and I nap a lot, mostly sleeping off my mini-hangovers. They're not real hangovers. I may just for once be getting genuinely tired with all the baby care and sneaking around. My boyfriend makes a lot of comments about how we're finally able to get proper rest far away from the city.

The weather is nice most of the time. It brings out the teenage surfers riding nonchalantly on boogie boards and probably praying for some kind of a storm to wipe all of us out, fat moms, and the few tourists, and for the waves to rise again.

———

A few times during the holiday I manage to buy some booze when we go grocery shopping. I tell my boyfriend I'll meet him inside the grocery store but instead I follow him to the liquor store first. He's a social drinker and likes his beer or wine with dinner.

As I follow him, the baby is rocked to sleep in his Snugli by my cat-like moves. I hide behind SUVs in the parking lot. Then I tiptoe through the sliding door into the liquor store entrance.

My boyfriend never looks behind him. The baby never makes a noise. I don't get caught.

Once my boyfriend leaves the liquor store, I slip inside.

Later, I pretend to run into the boyfriend somewhere in the cereal aisle, the newly purchased, full mickey safely tucked inside the diaper bag.

I dispose of empty mickey bottles in the bathrooms of back-road diners.

———

I never breastfeed when I drink. I make up some lie about nipples chafing. The baby is fed formula every other night. I drink every other night.

When I don't drink, I think about it.

I go through the day in a half-daze, thinking about it.

———

Because I don't drink as much as I would at home and I generally don't get too hungover after drinking, only once do I wake up sick enough to vomit into the toilet. When I was in my twenties, this used to be a point of pride. I'd translate from Polish the adage about being tough like a horse.

But that morning I wake up and it turns out I'm a very small pony. My stomach is upset, my skull is a vise to my pickled brain. Everything is squeezing from inside, begging to be expelled.

My boyfriend and the baby are still asleep in the bedroom when this happens. Just in case, I puke over my fist to mask the sound.

That day I sleep extra long on the beach. I forget the sunscreen and the sun is so intense, the redness comes on almost right away. My boyfriend is passed out beside me; the baby is in the wicker basket. We could just lie here on this nice beach and burn to a crisp, all three of us.

———

The boyfriend and I rarely fight during those two weeks, and I maintain the balance between tipsy and not-there perfectly well.

The baby smiles for the first time ever near the end of our two-week holiday. We've been waiting for him to smile, talking often about how he is due for it now, at three months old.

I'm hovering above him when it happens. My hair is long and sun-kissed with wispy ends. I move my head left to right, letting the wispy ends brush oh so gently over his beautiful, serious face. Back and forth. Back and forth.

Finally, something clicks. His eyes seem to focus, start moving back and forth with the wispy ends. The light is filtering through the window. His brown eyes, my brown eyes, the hair—we're a pendulum of the sun.

He smiles. The time stops. The pendulum stops: a baby just smiled for the first time ever somewhere in the world.

This is why we are all here on this planet, I think to myself.

We take hundreds of photos of him smiling.

REGROUP

When we get home, I start the harm reduction meetings. My boyfriend seems happy about it because he believes in education and therapy—he believes I will get educated enough about my own drinking to the point of stopping drinking. I keep insisting that I'm not that badly off that I would need to go back to AA. I don't need anything serious, like AA. Perhaps we both believe that I'm not that badly off.

There are ten of us in the group: three Robs, two Lisas, and a bunch of other clowns. I suppose I think of them as "clowns" because I'm hostile to this situation. And I'm not a clown myself. I'm here just to do some research. These people, on the other hand, need to be here. They are sad clowns. I am not.

The counselor, also a type of a clown, looks as if she hasn't smiled ever—her mouth has years and years of frowning etched into it. She gives us stickers with our names written on them and tells us to tell everyone what we're doing here.

We are in a classroom-like room and are, of course, seated in a circle, just like in the movies. I keep thinking: this is for them and not for me. In any event, if the clowns had any expectations of what this was supposed to look like, the hospital has done an excellent job of appropriating. Although I am thrilled to be in the movies. This is a movie.

Besides the circle, there's nothing much to look at. There are no paintings or photographs in this room, just us and the chairs and some tables pushed against the walls. The windows face a wall of another building.

In the beginning, everyone is silent. We look around, all of us, and smile quickly and politely at each other if we catch each other's eyes. Most of the eyes in here are accustomed to avoiding, so the awkward smiling occurs only a few times, at least in my case.

Eventually one of the Lisas bursts out that she doesn't even drink anymore so this program doesn't apply to her. Ever since her daughter moved back home with her new baby, well, she has realized how much was at stake and stopped drinking entirely.

No more drinking for her! Ha ha ha. It doesn't really apply at all, she repeats.

But I'm doing this—this program—because of the baby, she says. Because it's . . . it wouldn't be . . . it wouldn't be fair to him, the baby. If I did. Drink. Yes.

Lisa won't meet anyone's eye; she's playing with a loose thread coming out of her thick, wool skirt while she recites her affirmations.

Same with me, says the guy with the Einstein hairdo. Same with me. I don't even drink anymore. He gives everyone a sad, wise smile.

Well, good for you. An actor type with giant white runners on his feet shouts enthusiastically. But it hasn't been the case for me, certainly, he says. Good for you.

I went out last night, says the actor type. It was my last hurrah you could say. I understood that this is it for me. Or I don't know. I'm in a relationship and my girlfriend—we've been together twelve years—gave me an ultimatum. I usually drink Jack. I had some last night—

The counselor interrupts him to ask him how much.

He measures a depth with his hand. Almost an entire bottle from what I can tell. The counselor, visibly satisfied, nods and writes something down.

———

I wonder if I should take Lisa's approach when it comes to my turn and just make something up. Something about how I'm only here for the preventative measure or some other stupid crap. But I don't even care enough to lie all the way through.

I have to watch what I say, however. I was read a statement about confidentiality when I dropped off my form. I remember the words *danger* and *authorities*. This is no good. I can't talk about passing out with Frankie screaming and wet that one time, and my boyfriend finding me.

I just say that I drink because of the stress of childcare and my life, which is a failure.

I don't really attribute my drinking to this. I could talk about the obscene appetite of my wanting, or about the guilt crushing my sobriety, or perhaps about subconsciously wanting to die, not being able to stop. Yet all of that is too abstract, too complicated to explain. I can't explain it to *myself*. Why, Jowita? Why? I remember seeing a sticker once: The reason I swear so much is because fuck you.

But since I've been in this movie before, I know that you have to come up with some kind of explanation. Cause and effect. A formula that goes like this: Baby equals stress equals feeling of failure equals drinking.

So the childcare makes you stressed? the counselor says.

You know, like that joke title for a children's book? *Mommy Drinks Because You Cry*? That's me, I say.

The counselor doesn't laugh. Nobody laughs. Lisa looks at me suspiciously.

The counselor asks me where I drink. At home?

(I evaluate how I should answer. No. Not at home. Baby's at home, can't be drunk around the baby, can I?)

At a local bar.

How much do you drink?

A couple of pints.

How many?

Maybe two. Or three.

Two or three?

Three.

Four?

No, three.

The counselor tries to do something with her mouth that looks . . . smilish. I want to punch her. But I *smilish* back at her and she moves on to Lisa number two, who says she drinks to get herself to sleep. That, I think, is a terrible waste of being wasted.

I keep my mouth shut and look at the clock.

———

The last to introduce himself is one of the Robs. He looks like a middle-aged woman with short hair. He's got a soft chin and big green eyes, a strangely lumpy body and a big ass. He's the happiest-seeming out of the bunch. For sport, I try to figure him out quickly, before he gets to his story. I guess beers, mean ex-wife, divorced, a dad.

He says his name and where he's from. He's got a French accent. Quebec. Beers, divorced, a dad indeed. Nothing about the mean ex-wife but instead there's this bombshell: I'm an alcoholic, he says.

We don't label here, the counselor says. She looks like she would like to pat him on the back; she reassures him that he's no such thing. There are no alcoholics, schizophrenics or manic-depressives; there are just tendencies and behaviors, but no one is ever just his or her condition or addiction. There are so many different aspects to a person, so many different parts that make up an identity.

The counselor goes on about this for a little bit and then Rob cuts her off and says, But I identify as an alcoholic. That's my identity.

Fine, she says, but there's a frown on her forehead and I wonder if she's worried about the rest of us finding out that we too are alcoholics.

Indeed, as if on cue, Lisa announces that she's no alcoholic, she doesn't even drink, you know. Not since the baby. Not—

Rob sighs and says, But I am. I have to identify. I mean I don't have to—no one is forcing me—but I choose to. So I'm an alcoholic. I'd be drunk or dead without the meetings.

Yes, because the biggest joke is that he doesn't even drink. Hasn't had a drink for nine months, which is nothing, he assures us; there are people who have been sober for thirty years who still identify as alcoholics. But the real reason he's here, he says, is because of the outstanding court order.

I can't help but wonder if the real reason he's here, even subconsciously, is that he wants to feel a little superior. I imagine his nine-month-old sobriety is a speck of dirt compared to those thirty-year champions in Alcoholics Anonymous. Here, it must feel priceless to be able to say that he's an alcoholic who has been sober for longer than all of us added together.

———

In a way this place is a toy version of Alcoholics Anonymous. A Mickey Mouse club. A training ground for real group confessionals and serious recovery.

You clowns think this is difficult, Rob is possibly thinking. You should try doing this sort of thing ninety times in ninety days.

"Ninety in ninety" is what many new alcoholics do when they first get sober. It is not mandatory but it makes sense to do it. The mornings, afternoons or evenings of drinking get replaced with mornings, afternoons or evenings of church basements and bad coffee and immersion in the bizarre, outdated language of the Big Book, AA's official credo, first published in 1939.

And after the first ninety days it doesn't get that much easier. There are meetings every day, dozens of them throughout the day. Many people in AA will suggest the following math:

How many times in a week should I go to an AA meeting?

Well, how many times in a week do you drink?

Not that many people adhere to this formula, and it doesn't necessarily guarantee successful sobriety—nothing does, in fact—but it increases the chances of sobriety lasting.

————

If you think that AA is for the faint-hearted, for the broken losers of shaky hands, weak spines, think again. AA is rooms full of people who are living completely against their nature—the nature that requires them to drink and die. These are the proverbial fish out of water. And they are walking the earth, many of them walking it for years.

Unlike this harm reduction group, AA is a continuous program of recovery—there are no deadlines on your sobriety, no goals to set. If you're ready to go, you go. And once you go, there are people you can call, people you do call when the going gets tough. There are the twelve steps—suggested points on the map of recovery. But you only need to meet the first step to be a part of AA: admitting you are powerless over alcohol and that your life has become unmanageable.

There are many . . . questionable aspects of AA too. There can be prayers. There is lots of God. Officially there's no religion and no leader, but there's "one ultimate authority—a loving God as He may express Himself." And He does tend to be shoved down your throat.

This He is referred to as a "he." That can be a problem for some. Some may also find this god a little too Christian. After all, Alcoholics Anonymous's twelve steps have their roots in the Oxford

Group, a Christian fellowship that believed in confession being a prerequisite to change, the idea that a sinner could completely redeem herself.

AA is an institution set up and organized by people, so yes, it is imperfect. For that reason it is also full of people you have to put up with. People who have taken AA too far, people who decided that they have a monopoly on salvation. People who advise you on your health, your relationships, your diet. People without medical degrees who will eagerly tell you to get off your medication and pray instead. Who will suggest you read absurd self-help books, do yoga, go to sweat lodges. All of those things can help you live better, of course, but none of them have anything to do with AA. However, sometimes AA can feel like the emporium of all recovery for everything.

It is not.

But it is an emporium of sorts. AA refuses to call itself an organization, but it does have a type of constitution called "The Twelve Traditions." I am breaking one of its traditions right now: I'm telling you about AA.

Luckily, the most beautiful thing about AA is that even though I am breaking this tradition, I know that I can always, no matter what, go back to "the rooms"—what members call meetings—and that my fellow alcoholics will take me back with open arms and help me get sober.

Where this harm reduction group is just an evening class on addiction, AA is a full-time university program from which you never graduate.

Still, right now in this room, Rob seems like the smuggest of them all. Right now, Rob is symbolizing to me why I would never return to AA.

Back in the Mickey Mouse club, after the introductions we talk about our drinking habits and the strategies we can use to drink less or not drink at all. We look at a chart where a cartoon man is climbing a mountain, falling down, climbing back up, falling down. This is supposed to illustrate how one gets sober. The path isn't easy: you stumble many times before you get to the top.

Stumbling or slipping is part of recovery!!!, the cutline under the cartoon announces.

Which tells me that I could have a drink tomorrow. It's part of recovery.

———

In my pamphlet I change my goal from abstinence to max four drinks per week. Then I go over it with my pen to change the *4* to a somewhat square-looking *8*. Better. Better-looking, too.

———

Later, we do an exercise where we write down Trigger Situations and Solutions for how to deal with them.

My triggers: morning, evening, happy, sad, nothing, something.

You know, Lisa the liar blurts out, when I feel my cravings coming on I can just reach for a book. Not that I have cravings anymore but when I had them, I'd just read a short story by Alice Munro or something like that and poof, the craving is gone. But now with the baby I don't have as much time but I may still, you know, read a couple of lines here and there if I'm feeling a little anxious or something.

There isn't a writer in this world amazing enough to kill my cravings.

Another of the Robs tells us that he's about to become a father. His wife sent him here, he says, because she doesn't want a drunk to be her child's father. He's not sure if he's got a drinking problem. The counselor asks him to talk about his cravings, how often does he have them.

Once a day? he says.

She says, And for how long?

For as long as I'm awake, I answer her in my head.

He shrugs and says, I don't know, a couple of minutes.

Clearly satisfied, she writes it down in her notes. I wonder what she does with these notes later—does she translate all the numbers into averages and draw absurdly colorful pie charts at home?

And home, what is her home like? Is it a loud home with children's art on the walls? Does she get laid? Is there a guy or a girl who kisses her on her serious mouth, someone who likes to grab her from the back as she passes by and who likes to mess up the big bow on her pristine blouse?

———

During break, we go outside, just like you would if you were taking a course and it was a break and you needed a smoke. From outside, the addictions building looks like something on a university campus—nice yellow brick and glass and benches all around. If you weren't from around here, you could certainly be fooled into thinking this is a school. Until you look closer at the smokers and the people sitting on those benches and notice how they suck a little too hard on their cigarettes, or how their hair is matted, their mouths move without speaking, and the rounds of their irises flicker, or the opposite, stay almost completely still.

As soon as we're outside, I go up to almost-daddy Rob. I want to say *something* about being careful with the almost-baby and about my own relapse and how—I don't really know what. How hard it is? How strange it is? Either way, I don't really know why I want to talk to Rob and I don't really know what exactly my intentions are. It's not like anything I'll say will change his life, will sober him up, not like he and his wife will be able to return the baby to the store where they got him. I have no words of wisdom or warning for him but I stand there struggling, trying to come up with the right words, feeling like it's my responsibility to let him know everything about babies.

Forget sleeping, I say, lamely, and he pretends to laugh.

I relapsed shortly after I had my son, I add.

He looks at me, his face suddenly not friendly at all.

That's not what I'm trying to say. And it's not like you will relapse, right? Since you still drink. I mean, you can't relapse, right? Shit. Because you don't have a problem. No, I didn't mean it like that. Sorry.

No, it's okay, he says, but I can tell that he's pissed.

I want to do something to make up for my gaffe but I don't know what.

I wonder if he wants to sleep with me. Sure he wants to sleep with me. I could make an effort and flirt. But that's not it.

At last, it occurs to me. I offer him baby things.

I have everything, I say. A bouncy chair, a mobile, some awesome sleepers. You can have his tub, too. He doesn't need a tub, I mean he does but he's almost too big for it. And the mobile is just hanging there, right? It's a sheep mobile. I mean, it's little felt sheep with bells hanging off the branches. It's cute but he doesn't even use most of his stuff, I say, and in my mind strip my son's room of his things. I'm trying to be tougher than I really am. I am not that tough at all.

I think how it's true that Frankie possibly doesn't give a damn about the mobile, really, though how would I know what he thinks—he just lies there.

He just lies there?

No. I don't really think that. Even in my thinking I'm trying to show myself up. He doesn't just lie there. And now I have another thought: maybe the mobile is really special. Maybe it's so special that it's like god to him. The little felt sheep spinning slowly, the tinkling of bells creating a whole universe in front of my son's eyes. How would I ever know? I wouldn't know.

Rob looks at me without saying anything. I can't figure out the expression on his face.

Please speak, I ask in my head. But nothing.

Which is why I keep listing things: A milk warmer. It's pretty nifty. But we never use it. You don't have time to use most of this shit. When you're drunk ha ha ha. Shit, I mean, you would. *You* would have the time.

Okay.

Okay, I say back. Then I fall silent.

We finish our cigarettes in silence.

Well, I'll ask the wife if we need anything, he says, stiffly, and, stiffly, walks away.

———

The group meets for five weeks and I'm the only person who doesn't meet her goal (maximum eight drinks a week) and doesn't graduate. I have learned all of the program's tactics. I did all of the paper homework. On paper I am educated. And I must believe in magic because I expected to be transformed simply by taking the program. Yet, off paper, I fail every test.

———

I'm offered the one-on-one meetings with the thin-lipped counselor, which I attend twice, both times with the baby so that I have the excuse to leave sooner.

HOW TO GET RID
OF BOTTLES

Though I have taken the course on self-improvement and harm reduction, it seems that my life continues to get more complicated, difficult to manage.

For example, getting rid of the bottles becomes an issue.

Somehow there are always too many of them, and even though I'm quite disciplined about their removal, they keep showing up unexpectedly, as if they had been breeding somewhere.

Instead of the one that I remember, suddenly three, and a plastic screw-top from a mickey, emerge from the depths of my closet. Underneath the shoe rack there is another one. Sometimes the unexpected squashed face of a beer can will reveal itself.

———

I put the bottles and cans and caps that I find into a plastic bag and I shove that into the diaper bag, cover it with the package of wipes to make sure no one—the boyfriend—will find it. I can't get caught with the empties.

Because there are no empties.

I'm not drinking. Despite being a Centre for Addiction and Mental Health alumna now and despite the bottles, there is a part of me that tells myself this: I'm not drinking. And I believe myself most of the time, truly.

———

Besides garbage cans, I leave the plastic bags in bushes, recycling bins in front of houses, public bathrooms. I'm the reverse of the people you sometimes see in the morning with shopping carts filled with glass, looking in the garbage, the bins. If I were better organized I could probably find my own bottle collector, someone to relieve me of this little chore.

Sometimes, when I'm walking, I turn right into a private driveway as if I were about to visit the people who live here. I stop, crouch beside the stroller as if to tie a shoe or check on the baby. In one well-oiled move, I grab the plastic bag and lay it on the ground like some kind of mutant egg, and then get up, turn around and walk away.

I can't properly relax until I get rid of the empties. I can sense them, as if they are embedded in me somewhere, their presence pulsating underneath the surface.

I try to never repeat the disposal site, and as time goes on I have to walk for miles before I have a chance to get rid of my empties. Occasionally, miraculously, I forget about them, and when I reach into the diaper bag to get my son's bottle of milk and my hand brushes against the rustle of the plastic, I panic.

And I also wish my hand to wilt right then and there.

———

The city installs a new type of garbage can to replace the old bins. They fill up extremely quickly, and by mid-afternoon trash is being shat out of the holes right onto the ground. The bins are often found near bus or streetcar stops, dirtying up everything around them. You always have to squash your garbage to get it inside. Even with meticulously crushed cans or slick, flat shapes of mickeys tightly wrapped in plastic, you can't just slip them in. I often give up, afraid that someone will notice my struggle. Streetcars keep coming, with people trickling out of them, making me jumpy.

But a few times I don't walk away. I wait for whatever streetcar to start moving and then I take out the plastic bag, perversely slowly, and start stuffing it into the garbage. Doing this, I look up, stare right back at them, the people behind the glass of the streetcar.

A few times I even take the bottles out of the plastic—inspired by my own shittiness, perhaps I want to shame myself further: Yes, it's an empty bottle of wine you're looking at. And yes, I'm throwing it out here, in public, instead of at home. And yes, that's a baby in the stroller.

The streetcars keep on moving.

And later, once all of the evidence—the bottles—is gone, I will again tell myself that none of this had happened and that there's nothing wrong with me.

———

There are other bottles too that I have to get rid of. In my sad world these bottles are inexplicably related to the first kind of bottles. Because of the first type, I end up buying a lot of formula.

Premixed, it comes in cans, or, for more money, you can buy it in twist-top glass bottles. The bottled brand is Good Start, and I don't know if I should take its name as the biggest irony or the biggest salvation.

I don't like using Good Start but I use it often. I use it when my milk turns to poison and when I haven't been able to save enough of my own supply.

I buy it all the time just in case anyway.

I'm sick. I'm responsible.

———

I'd always planned to breastfeed exclusively. But that was before I relapsed. When I still had some idea of how this was supposed to look: A baby's face pressed against the swelling chest. Beatific smile on my face.

Indeed, I loved the idea of being able to be the only food source for my child. And it was never discussed that his feeding would happen any other way. I was given books with titles like *The Womanly Art of Breastfeeding*.

The doctors suggested signing up for breastfeeding classes.

———

I spent the first three weeks of my son's life grinding my teeth in pain from cracked, bleeding nipples because I neglected to read the books and I wasn't paying attention in classes.

Once my son latched on properly, however, it was heavenly. I had experienced pleasure so deep, it felt pre-orgasmic. With every gulp, we were re-establishing our connection outside of the womb, and it was the most intimate, sacred relationship I've ever had. A self-proclaimed agnostic, I was convinced I could hear the angels sing when he fed. His mouth was a portal to the universe.

So I went ahead and I destroyed that connection.

———

When my drinking becomes a regular occurrence, I start looking up charts online to figure out how much time it takes for the alcohol to leave my body. Not a lot of alcohol from each drink gets into breast milk, but babies are small and the drinks are many.

With my body weight and the amounts I consume, I calculate I need nine to fourteen hours before the alcohol completely clears out of my system. Sometimes more.

I let a lot of the milk into the sink in an exercise referred to as "pump and dump" by mommies online. Mommies who perhaps have had one too many Green Appletinis at a Christmas party. Mommies who, I presumed, would never consider integrating "pump and dump" into their daily schedule.

I buy breast pumps. Yes, plural—I buy three.

I also learn how to milk myself by hand.

I figure out a few magic hours during the day when I can do it and I store the milk in the diaper bag for later. I bring earlier-prepared bottles with me on my walks.

I hide those too. I hide everything.

———

Furthermore, I set secret alarms on my laptop to let me know when the time is up. Once my milk is safe to be consumed, I feed my son. With Good Start to supplement him, he is probably the most over-fed baby in the city.

But if he is too full and refuses to eat, I save the milk for later. I become very good at expressing milk in bathrooms of coffee shops, my nipple pressed against the plastic of the baby bottle, my fingers squeezing in the correct engorged places, the bottle, mercifully, filling up.

———

Stopping breastfeeding means admitting to the fact that there is a problem and that I am failing as a mother.

It is harder for me to deny to myself that I am a premeditated drinker. That although I don't intend to drink, if alcoholism was murder I'd be charged on the first degree.

But I continue to engage in doublethink. There's a problem no there isn't a problem there is a problem no there isn't.

———

In the safe hours of the day, I breastfeed my son confidently and happily. Those are the only times when I feel like a full-on parent. I am the parent I expected myself to be. That everyone expects me to be. This is my only period of grace.

———

And do I always succeed in not breastfeeding my son while under the influence?

No.

I cannot with full certainty say that I always manage to wait enough time before I put him up to my breast after my mandatory nine to fourteen hours of rest. Sometimes less time passes.

I try very hard, but trying very hard is just that: trying very hard.

I try very hard.

And there are a few times I am acutely aware of less time passing but I breastfeed him because of my lying—I know that people around me won't accuse me of drinking the night before if I breast-feed him.

———

I don't ask for help because I am scared. Also too proud. Admitting I am in trouble doesn't mean asking for help—it means asking to be shunned. Am I not the queen of this country? Don't the people trust me with ruling it responsibly and with love? Don't they ask me to stop being destructive? Am I not given a hundred chances? Asking for help means there will be consequences and they will be dire.

My mind, fogged with drink, anxiety and mental illness, tells me the worst. For example, I often envision my boyfriend packing my bags, kicking me out to live on the street. Seeing police cars on the street can mean I am about to go to jail. My sister's worried mouth means she is secretly plotting to have me locked up in a psych ward.

This is not me.

Me? I am just a mom.

I want so badly to be a good mom.

Please, don't get mad, look at me, I'm doing it, I'm doing it—I'm being a mom!

And I hope that maybe they are thinking: We're not mad. We're not sending her away. She is. A mom. She wouldn't do *that* to her child, would she?

She would.

She does.

I'm guilty. If not of murder, I'm guilty of manslaughter. As the legal definition has it: "It is not always obvious whether a killing is murder or manslaughter. Many times, the difference is based on what the accused was thinking at the time of the death, which can be extremely difficult to prove in court."

I'm turning myself in. I'm turning myself in because I'm pathetic and because of another paradox: I am trying to be a responsible drunk mom and I fail at that too.

So the other containers I often get rid of along with the empties are the bottles of formula that I buy on my walks to the local drug-stores.

Officially, we have cans of premixed formula at home, but I am so paranoid about alcohol getting into the breast milk (always trying, always failing, always guilty over failing) that I buy extras all the time. I don't want my boyfriend to see how many extras I go through. He would ask questions.

My checking account is often near zero. The formula is pricey. I think of how pricey it is when I buy it. I don't think about my checking account being near zero when I'm in the liquor store. I don't think how pricey vodka is when I buy it. Priorities.

Secret extras of Good Start in the fridge behind vegetables.

Secret singles of Good Start in my son's diaper drawer.

Empties in plastic bags. On the bottom of the stroller. Breeding in my closet.

I can't keep away from bottles. I obsess over them. I am the Howard Hughes of bottles.

I am the Howard Hughes of secrets.

RATS AND COCAINE

One night in September, my sister comes over to help with the baby. She is in her final year at school, so her schedule is hectic, but I appreciate any help I can get. I'm feeling lonely too. Even though I'd never admit it to myself, that's what it is, loneliness.

He's asleep, I tell my sister. So no worries, I say, channeling someone, not sure who. Someone who worries not.

I offer her some orange juice; have a glass of it too. I have to keep a close eye on my glass. I mixed my juice with white wine earlier. She would never grab it and try to smell it. Still, I keep a close eye on the glass.

You okay? my sister says and looks at me in that way she looks at me.

Of course I'm okay. I just said no worries, no?

She says nothing.

I'm fine, I say one more time.

I love my sister. She's so awesome. She should stop writing me letters though about how much my relapse hurts her.

Okay, she says.

Listen, there are no secrets with me. Everything's out in the open. We can talk about it. I want to talk about it. I want to bring it up. Right now.

She says right now may not be the best time.

Why? Now is as good time as any.

She looks at me in that way she looks at me, again.

She's younger than me. I practically raised her.

I just don't understand it, she says. I want to understand.

Understand. What's there to understand.

She says nothing. Then: I should probably go.

Wait. Wait, I almost scream. I've got an idea.

I run around pulling books off shelves looking for all the addiction memoirs and that book about neurological causes of addiction.

I want to read some important passages from this book to her, but can't find the good stuff about rats and cocaine. The pages seem to be all smeared with bouncy letters. The paragraphs are wavy as if melting off the paper.

Maybe she will have more luck with it.

I lay the book on my sister's lap and tell her to look for it. Find the stuff about rats and cocaine, I urge her. Check the index in the back for rats and cocaine. Read the whole book. Have it. You can borrow it. No, have it. It's yours.

She says she has no time to read huge books about addiction. She is in grad school.

Hold that thought, I tell her and run upstairs.

———

Upstairs, it is quiet. The baby is sleeping.

I check on him to make sure.

I also check in the drawer where I keep the diapers.

Once I check on the baby and behind the diapers, I run back downstairs to talk at my sister some more. I cut her off when she starts talking gibberish again. When am I going to get better? What's wrong?

Let me finish, let me finish, I keep saying to her, as if "let me finish" was some kind of abracadabra that would give me an infinite right to go on and on and make her shut up.

Somewhere in the back of my drunk's reptile brain I know that I'm being obnoxious, but I have so much to teach her. As her older and more experienced sister it truly is my duty to teach her about life. She has to learn about addictions. I am probably an addict. Though I'm almost sober now. But I want someone to understand. Is this too much to ask?

I speak in capital letters, feeling my conviction fill me up as if I were a balloon. I mention the rats and the cocaine again because I don't think she got it the first time. It is imperative that she understands how those things work.

So. The rats and cocaine.

The rats that lived in dire conditions were way more likely than the rats that lived in the so-called Rat Park (Rat Park. I remember the name of the experiment, so I shout it) to self-administer drugs. Drugs didn't cause addiction. The past did. Circumstances.

I grab the book from her lap.

The text seems more cooperative now. I even find the quote I've been looking for and kept missing for some reason. I read it triumphantly to my sister: "Only severely distressed animals, like severely distressed people, will relieve their distress pharmacologically if they can."

My sister says, Okay, and then, out of the blue: Are you drinking? Are you drunk now?

You're such an idiot, I tell her.

She really is.

———

I run upstairs, back into the baby's room. I fish the mickey out of the diaper drawer—it is almost empty now, crap—and take another swig.

COSMOPOLITAN

There is a vague idea in my head about a woman that I want to emulate. In my delusion, I believe that I'm qualified to practice being her, precisely because I drink.

This woman, she travels first-class and stays at boutique hotels. She is unapproachable, on the verge of being mistaken for a former model, or, if you aren't entirely convinced about her beauty, the way she carries herself at least suggests she's important. This woman is very much in control of herself and her confidence is natural, not cocky, but if you find it a bit cocky she certainly doesn't care what you think.

This is the woman who's going to Montreal for a fun weekend. It's fall but it's still warm out, perfect weather for sophisticated travel. I booked her trip months ago. It was a birthday gift from my boyfriend who is staying home with the baby while the woman travels.

———

Walking, I make her legs line up one behind the other, making her pelvis bounce just a tad too much. You have to look once you notice her—you have to look one more time to make sure you aren't missing something. And then you are left feeling that you did, indeed, miss something.

She walks into the lobby of the hotel carrying a small, sexy suitcase packed only with a little black dress, high-quality stockings, lingerie and stilettos. In the lobby, the woman gives the receptionist my boyfriend's credit card and in exchange receives a card key and complimentary art-museum passes given to all the guests.

The elevator going up plays tranquil music. The walls are wallpapered and mirrored; there is information about yoga classes, the spa and other services. It is unclear whether there is a pool in the hotel.

I look back at the woman's reflection in the mirror. Her eyes are a little tired and there are bags underneath them. The baby had been waking up throughout the night for the last few nights straight, prior to this trip. Four, five times a night. The breasts feel full of milk. *My* breasts feel full of milk. I milked myself on the train earlier but the milk is now back, expanding inside them, probably starting to leak out and right into my brand-new lace bra.

And like that, I am no longer her, I am me again, a mom with leaky tits.

———

The hotel room is a heavy-wood wallpapered coffin with an enormous bed. I unpack the little suitcase and check out the tray of heavily priced objects in shiny packages on the desk. Dental dam? Never seen one in a hotel before. Never seen one, period.

I sit on the bed and watch a show about renovating houses while I milk myself.

After I shower and dress, I'm ready to be *her* again.

I take some pictures of her. On the camera's viewscreen they show just the right amount of blurry gold hair, black dress, fuchsia tights and crossed legs against the dark bed covers. It all seems intriguing, illicit. Blurry enough to miss the dark circles under the eyes.

———

She walks out of the hotel in search of a bar. Behind the hotel, the streets seem populated with drunk children. All the bars she passes look horrible. Even the more elegant ones are occupied by the sort of male who likes to show off the top of his chest and the sort of long-haired female who is often blond and tanned as if she spent her summers in a warm place where the air smells of coconut.

There is loud music everywhere and people are puking on street corners.

The men catcall and look at the woman even with all the fresh flesh around her. She wants to be left alone, however, so she walks briskly and grows more and more frustrated, trying to find the perfect place to drink.

There is, finally, a horrible but relatively empty dark pub where I find a quiet corner and knock down four pints in a row. I've never had this kind of beer, Amsterdam Blonde; beer isn't exactly what *she* should be drinking but *I* am a beer drinker so I make her disappear. She can come back tomorrow when I have more time to plan what to do with her and her sophisticated tastes. The TV is on in the corner, there are American accents all around me, and nobody is looking at me, except for the bartender—which is all that matters anyway.

I drink the beer fast. I don't want to stay here for too long—there's too much to do outside.

But I'm in the wrong part of town to do things. I should be closer to St-Denis. I'm not familiar with the city but surely I can find a place more interesting than this pub. So I leave, and wander the awful streets around Rue Ste-Catherine, looking inside bars, trying to find one where I can finish off my evening, drink myself sober.

I finish my evening at a Korean restaurant where I have to buy food to go with my beer. I ask for soybeans. The kid serving me seems scornful when I order a third beer. He asks me in broken English if I want anything else to eat besides soybeans.

Why? Is he worried about my health? I hate these stupid soybeans but no, I don't want anything else. And I hate this beer, as a matter of fact. And this restaurant. Does he think I want to be here? Really? That out of the entire, beautiful city of Montreal, I picked this basement to spend the rest of my night—here, where nobody seems to be speaking English?

No more food, I'm fine, I bark.

He blinks at all of this and bows his head and walks away.

I'm alone at the table. The other four tables are jammed with beautiful Asian kids giggling and flirting among themselves, ignoring me completely. Perhaps they are giggling at me the entire time.

———

The next morning I wake up sore and angry at the world in my ridiculous huge bed. The sheets are stained with milk.

———

The second night she is much more prepared. First of all, she bought a nice bottle of wine earlier, which she drinks in the hotel room while watching a TV show about adopted children reuniting with their biological parents. It's a good show.

She dances a little in the small room, as much as she can, really, in this room. She has to maneuver around the bed. Dancing, she thinks about the time long ago when she used to date a very rich guy who would take her to hotels like this. He would leave at one in the morning to drive back to his wife and daughter. And she would sometimes wake up too early, very thirsty suddenly, and she would crack open the mini-fridge. Those hotels were like this one—all wood, sometimes all glass, ambient techno in the elevators and faux Deco decor.

When she finishes her bottle of wine, she puts on more lipstick and goes downstairs to the hotel restaurant, which is arctic blue and black with skating-rink-shiny surfaces that seem to be made out of onyx. She orders a glass of wine. The glass costs more than the bottle she drank upstairs but she can't think that way—people like her don't have to think that way. It never occurs to them to be thrifty.

The girl behind the bar is very beautiful. The woman tells her this and the bartender girl says thank you. The woman orders another glass of wine and this time leaves a larger tip. The bartender seems so nice. The woman feels like talking so she starts a conversation with the bartender. It turns out that the bartender is a student at McGill, finishing the same degree as the woman's younger sister. What a coincidence. The bartender has smooth, pharaoh-like features, accented perfectly by only a hint of makeup.

The woman's purse vibrates and rings.

It's my boyfriend: How is Montreal?

Montreal is great. I'm having so much fun, I say and gulp the last few drops, gesturing to the beautiful bartender for another one. How is the baby?

He's good. A little cranky. He slept in our bed last night. I couldn't get him back to sleep so I let him. I guess all the sleep training just went out the window.

My boyfriend has some people over. Women friends. I ask him to list them. Among them is the friendly lady who's been pursuing him for months, someone he has had a drink with before (business reasons, of course), and this bothers me, but I'm suddenly in such a generous spirit I almost tell him that he can sleep with her if he really wants to. Why the hell not? People should be allowed to bang whoever they want. I know she wants to bang him. I know men like to sleep with people who want to sleep with them. So why not?

Stop being crazy. How was your day? he says, interrupting my thoughts.

I have a big sip of my wine and tell him about my hotel room and about the boring art I saw earlier. I don't tell him that I had been counting down the minutes until it would get dark and I could give myself permission to get drunk.

We miss you, Mommy, he says and puts the baby on the phone. I listen to the squeals and piglet-like grunting and I imagine my baby boy's little face with its giant inquisitive eyes, and his fists sometimes moving up to his eyes involuntarily, possibly trying to scratch them out.

I look at the rows of bottles in front of me. All the colors of glass and all that liquid; potions and lotions to make you big or small.

The bartender's back is turned to me now—she is pouring amber liquid into a row of tumblers. Her hair is black, shiny like the onyx surfaces around me. She probably wears matching microfiber-and-lace underwear.

One of the male waiters joins her behind the bar and she goes on her tippytoes to whisper something into his ear. I wonder if they are sleeping together. How do people ask to sleep with each other nowadays? I wonder how I would ask him to sleep with me.

I miss you too, guys, I say.

He wants to grab the phone, my boyfriend says. Oh, he's grabbing it, trying to hold it against his ear. Frankie! I hear the baby make a giggling sound.

Frankie. I can't think about Frankie right now. Hello? Hello? I say loudly into my cell.

My boyfriend says, Hello, hello, hello. What's wrong? Can you not hear me okay? I can hear you fine.

Hello? Hello? I say again.

Hello? I can hear you perfectly clearly.

Hello? Hello? I hang up.

He is ruining my buzz.

———

This time she doesn't go behind the hotel, back to the college-kid purgatory. Instead, she walks along Sherbrooke, passing the handsome facades, display windows and work-of-art staircases of expensive shops. She passes a couple of hotels with famous names. There are very few people out at this time. It seems that everyone has already retired for the night. A few hotel restaurants that she passes seem barely filled. It's past suppertime. It's getting chilly. It's Sunday.

She realizes that she is a little hungry, which is annoying. She should've had something to eat before. Maybe even a sandwich that she could've smuggled into her room like the nice wine. Nobody needed to know.

She stops in front of a couple of restaurants and reads the menus. The prices are ridiculous. Yes, she wants to treat herself, and women like her eat alone in expensive restaurants all the time, but this is just a rip-off. It's time to catch a cab and go down to St-Denis. There, at least, people are out on the streets and there are depanneurs everywhere, still probably selling alcohol at this hour.

One more place to check out. Last night on her way to the hotel she walked by this place and there was a big party inside a big white tent set up in the courtyard. People were all dressed up, and there were cameras inside, and a live band. There was wrought iron, possibly a fountain in the middle of all this, palm trees. It seemed like something out of *The Great Gatsby*.

The place is way less lively now.

She walks up to the restaurant's massive front door with curlicue knobs. The menu is framed in an intricate art nouveau frame.

The door opens and a man says hello.

Hello.

Would you like to come in? He is dressed in a suit. He's older than her but not by much. He's okay to look at, tanned and dark-haired, which she likes, but somehow not her type at all. He reminds her of a nice guy she went on a date with once, and kissed out of politeness.

The restaurant is empty behind the man.

She isn't sure what to make of it.

We're closed but you can come in. I saw you walking up and I was hoping you'd come in. I love your tights.

She looks down. Her fuchsia legs. Behind her, the street is deserted. Why the hell not?

This is how magic happens, she thinks. You have a drink or two and magic just happens.

————

The man leads her to a table and explains that he is the owner of the place. He says, I want to cook for you. It's not every day that such a beautiful woman just appears at my door.

She laughs.

Minutes later, she's seated at a white table, suddenly surrounded by eager-to-please waiters, and the man is telling her about different wines they have and what is good. She tries to remember what kinds of wines are considered good. Her mind is blank and a little whirly. She tells him to choose. I trust you, she says, and that seems to please him.

What would you like to eat? I can make you a beautiful salad.

I love salads, she says.

It shows. You have an amazing body, he says.

It's a little cheesy but she says thank you. Someone like her would always say thank you.

He jokes with the waiters, who call him "boss" and who are told to take out salad ingredients and leave them out for him in the kitchen. He wants to talk about her tights again. Her dress is beautiful too. What is she doing here, all by herself?

The wine is really good.

There is more of it.

She tells him he looks like an old friend.

A *good* friend? he wants to know.

An ex-boyfriend, she lies.

By then the surroundings are becoming seriously blurry. He looks like her ex-boyfriend, sure. Anybody could look like—or be—anybody. She keeps forgetting the man's name and once calls him by the name of the guy that he reminds her of. He jokes about having his feelings hurt, reminds her of his real name.

———

Later on a college-age kid joins them. He's wearing a pink Lacoste shirt. He was playing golf all day, he explains to the restaurant owner. He says he is enjoying himself after breaking off his engagement. They drink to that. The kid is the restaurant owner's nephew. They are Italian.

She calls them mafia and the restaurant owner laughs and the younger man rolls his eyes. The restaurant owner says he is going to go and make her salad now. It's a good thing, she thinks—food—as she's getting way too drunk.

The kid asks questions. He seems suspicious of her.

———

His suspicions make me nervous. I'm a mom, I finally tell him, losing my disguise.

A mom? And where's your husband? the kid asks.

The restaurant owner comes back with the salad. There are strawberries in it and walnuts. It's a strange salad, not very good, but at this point I would eat anything.

As I eat, the kid explains to the restaurant owner that I'm a new mom and the restaurant owner says that there's no way I'm a mom. I don't look like a mom.

Well, I am a mom, I say. Thank you.

Are we going? says the kid. They have plans.

Maybe not now, says the restaurant owner. He talks about my tights to the kid, who seems unimpressed.

What was your former fiancée like? I ask the kid. I try to picture the girl whom he dumped. She probably looked like one of those girls from the streets behind my hotel, from the night before. One of those puking-on-the-corner California girls. She probably had blond hair.

She was a knockout, the kid says.

Was? Is she dead?

He says, Yes, was.

Ah. Mafia. Where were you gonna go tonight? I say. I'm almost done my salad. I have more wine. The waiter brings another bottle.

I really want a cigarette. Can I smoke in here?

The restaurant owner doesn't answer right away. Then he says to the kid, Look, see how much I'm into this woman? I'm going to let her smoke in here.

I light a cigarette. Where were you gonna go, guys? I ask again, and the kid laughs but nothing in his face looks smiley.

Clubs. You know.

Strip clubs? I say, because it's obvious. I can come with you, I don't care. I love them. I went this summer and had a great time. I got a lap dance and everything. I went for a friend's birthday. Your ex didn't deserve you, I say. My voice probably gets higher and I flap my eyelashes.

No, she didn't. How was the lap dance?

It was great. The stripper was great. Beautiful. She looked like me.

I can get a driver to take us there. We'll go to my club, the restaurant owner says, and the young man nods knowingly.

Do you do other things? I ask.

They both laugh. Like what?

Mafia things. Never mind.

More wine. I have another cigarette. The restaurant owner tries to kiss me after that and I push him away, playfully. He says, I'm getting you drunk. There is more wine.

And then there's nothing.

———

I wake up in my hotel room. My underwear is off but my bra is on. It's completely soaked through with milk. There is nothing missing from my purse. The restaurant owner's business card is lying on the floor beside my tights.

I try to imagine the rest of the evening. Dancing? Falling?

Nothing seems to bring back any memories. Did I say offensive things to those men? I recall calling them mafia. I think I have one memory of passing out in the restaurant and them trying to wake me up . . . but this isn't a memory; it is just something that I guess.

Did they carry me back to my room? Did they have to ask at the front desk which one was my room? Did we actually go to Rue Ste-Catherine and visit a strip club after all? Did I invite them here, both of them, and did we have a threesome? Did the restaurant owner undress me, roll down those dirty, fuchsia tights slowly and lovingly, take pictures of me, while his nephew watched, impatient and fed up with this drunken slob his uncle was so taken with? Did they both see my C-section scar and realize that I wasn't the woman they thought I was? That I was indeed who I said I was—a new mom, staying in Montreal for the weekend, visiting art galleries and drinking too much wine. Why am I not wearing any underwear?

———

I don't think anything bad happened.

Perhaps all that happened was wobbly, stumbly me getting walked to my hotel room, being let in, put to bed. Maybe I wobbly, stumbly walked myself to the hotel room, let myself in, put myself in bed. I took my own clothes off.

The end.

———

But the truth is, I don't know for sure.

My blackouts are the perfect, absolute erasers of reality. There are no maybes, no gray edges. It's pure temporary death. And not the death that ends with a warm light at the end of the tunnel. Not even flickering. No flashbacks coming back later, either.

People don't believe in the absoluteness of blackouts. Perhaps because we simply don't accept that we can be here, on earth, walking and talking and doing things without any of it being recorded somewhere, kept to be released later.

But no light comes on, ever. From my end this is what it looks like: An alcoholic drinks and drinks, she goes into a blackout and then it's a long nothing and then she is waking up and it's the middle of the day. The carnage of fuchsia pantyhose, shoes, underwear strewn all around her with no clues as to the sequence of events preceding this.

———

I've heard of extraordinary fits, of alcoholics traveling to different countries in blackouts. I've heard of an alcoholic judge who left his own wedding in Ontario and woke up in a bed in Alberta with two strange women. I've heard of a man who came to and found he was delivering his daughter.

It is terrifying shit.

I don't think I was molested.

The end.

———

I decide to leave. I start packing. I find my panties in the bathtub. I throw them out. In the garbage there's the dental dam wrapper. Perhaps I unwrapped it last night, looked at it. The end.

———

I check out nervously, worried that someone is going to make a remark about the night before, tell me that I had damaged something, that maybe I threw up all over the elevator, maybe tried to make out with the waiter from the hotel bar that I thought of sleeping with earlier.

Nobody says anything.

I drag my suitcase out onto the sidewalk. I'm too mortified to walk by the restaurant, so I catch a cab and get to the train station hours before my train leaves. I remember a liquor store nearby—I passed it on my first day here. I drag my suitcase all the way there and buy a mickey of vodka. Even though I'm not drinking it (yet), knowing that I have it immediately calms me down.

———

In the train station food court only one bar is open. It's a dark, dank sports bar, a baseball game all round me on the screens suspended from the ceiling, and a carpeted floor littered with white flecks, possibly peanut shell remnants.

I order a pint of beer.

WHY

Believe me, I tried to figure out why. Why, for example, one warm fall evening, I somehow end up in Chinatown at the end of a busy shopping trip, and why I push my tired body and the tired stroller forward, pretending to be here to find a scarf.

In reality, I am here so that I can stumble upon a liquor store. The one close to Kensington Market, one I've never been to but that I've been aware of, of course. I pretend that this is a total surprise when I do walk by it.

What was that?

Was that?

Imagine that! A liquor store.

I walk a bit longer and then turn around. I could get some wine to go with my dinner tonight. The boyfriend is away at some conference—we decided that it makes sense for him to go away now to get a break after my Montreal trip. It's my turn to be with the baby all by myself.

I don't mind at all. Tonight I will cook myself a nice meal, treat myself. Maybe I should get a pedicure. Rent a funny movie about blondes getting married to their best friends whom they never saw in a romantic light until the high school reunion. Call my best friend in Poland. Make it a night.

I go inside.

I had no idea that the store has a flight of dangerously high stairs. Ridiculous. There's no ramp. There is a wheelchair lift, a tiny platform that I step onto and then have to shut the little doors behind me before it will move. You can move it with either a manual handle or by pressing a big red button with the words UP/DOWN printed on it. The lift makes a loud noise, and moves slowly, in full view of everyone in the store. It's actually performance art, this indiscreet and attention-seeking hulk of ancient machinery going up with me standing right in the middle of it.

Once we get out of the lift, I imagine that I can feel people watching us.

I know what this looks like. This is exactly what it looks like, although, naturally, I'm pretending otherwise. But if you need to know the truth: Yes, I am ashamed to be here with a stroller. And I don't know why I'm here, buying a bottle of wine and also—why not?—a mickey of vodka, telling myself that I'm just buying it for tonight's special dinner, that I will only have one glass of wine—max two.

No more than three.

But, in the back of my mind, I know already that I won't just have a glass or three. I will have the entire bottle. Then I'll drink the mickey. Then I'll run frantically around the house trying to find anything else that will give me a buzz. On not finding anything, I will have a thought to run out of the apartment, just for a bit, not long at all, and go to the nearest bar and down a quick pint.

The baby will be fine in his crib; it's not like I'm going to be gone long. Yes, I know that there's a Murphy's Law about accidents and babies left alone, which is why I never leave Frankie alone. Even in a state of the most profound drunkenness I am always somehow able to talk myself out of this idea—usually by passing out—and stay at home, avoiding disaster.

But I am scared.

My fear is that one day the perfect combination of insanity and alcohol will cause me to ignore the last-ditch responsible thought and I *will* leave and drink at the bar only to come back to one of these: a house on fire, the baby suffocated by a blanket, the baby face down in his own puke.

And yet, knowing all this, having fast-forwarded the tape all the way through to the end, I have just marched through this Chinatown liquor store and found the wine and the vodka.

———

The cashier says, How old is the baby?

The baby? I mumble something about having a dinner party and a lot of friends over, never answering her question, never even hearing her question, until I'm back on the wheelchair lift that is slowly, shamefully, grunting its way down. I hear it then, an echo in my head. I answer it in my head.

He's five and a half months old.

The next day I wake up on the loveseat in the living room with my neck stiff, shoes on. I can't remember what happened last night.

He is in his crib, asleep, looking peaceful and fat. Bottles of formula spill milk onto the mattress. He's got enough formula in there to drown in. What a responsible mother I am.

Once I'm downstairs in the kitchen I discover that there was no dinner. No food to make dinner with. There are bottles wrapped in newspapers ready to be taken out and disposed of later.

I make a decision to stay home until the boyfriend gets back. I'm mortified by the fact that I drank without anyone around to take care of the baby in case I drank myself to death, fell on my head or choked on vomit. I'm so mortified, my immediate thought is to drink this shame out of me, but I manage to resist. I can't risk it anymore. This means a week without alcohol. But the fear of dying and worse, finding my son dead, is suddenly a siren, not just a weak little buzz in the back of my head.

I sleep a lot.

On day three I wake up sweaty—and proud—as if I had run a marathon. I'm not hungover. I breastfeed all the time now, and Frankie's happy despite the snotty nose and a little bit of a cough. We spend most of our days in bed, both of us gurgling and chatting and laughing, his fat feet kicking madly, sometimes landing on my battered body, but I don't mind.

We take a bath together. He pees in the tub; this makes me chuckle hard and he looks up at me and joins me, mouth opening in a laugh so powerful that it doesn't make a lot of sound, except for one loud *hyeee* that comes out of him when he inhales deeply. He smacks one of my collarbones and his mouth turns upside down in surprise. I can tell he has hurt himself, but I distract him from crying, make a high-pitched noise, something between a scream and a coo. He looks at me uncertainly. Then he laughs again through the beginning of his tears. I feel like I'm god.

Drying myself, I look in the bathroom mirror. I'm getting skinny. I'm running out of whatever food I do have, so I may have to leave the house after all. I try not to think about it. Today will be one more day eating out of cans and I'll love it—anything to not have to leave.

As I pat my sweet baby-boy dry, I kiss him all over his bean-shaped belly, kiss him on the soles of his fat feet.

I feel I've never been happier.

After our bath, we lie down.

———

I read.

Three days sober, I read like I drink. The right side of the bed—my side—is heaped with books and magazines. I have many different subscriptions and I buy books all the time, but I'm usually too drunk to read. Now, between sleeps, baths and heating up cans, I read. I go through all kinds of inspiring stories in women's magazines, a few short stories from recent issues of *The New Yorker*, two novels and a non-fiction book about genetic disorders. I am learning so much. I'm hoping that Frankie is sucking in all that knowledge with the breast milk. It feels as though we are both detoxifying from the debilitating past few months.

———

The next day it's beautiful outside but I daren't go out even after I discover that all the cans are definitely gone. I know that I need to eat—for both of us—but I'm so terrified of what will happen outside that I'm actually considering starving to death. I'm not being dramatic—I do think about it. I think about calling my sister, asking her to come down at the end of the week so that she can find Frankie, still alive, ready to be rescued. I imagine him stuck to my dead breast sucking the final drops, surviving. But what if he doesn't?

———

I search online for "How long does it take to starve to death?" and am told it "depends on several factors such as your weight and how healthy you are. Most medical doctors state you can live four to six weeks without food. Some obese people have been known to live up to 25 weeks without food, but you can only live three days without water, except for some rare cases where people have lived 8–10 days without water."

Three days if without water. I could do it. I've three days left exactly.

Of course, I'm not entirely serious about starving myself to death and you absolutely have to be serious in order to be successful in such an endeavor. Which means that sooner or later I'll have to go out.

———

If I go outside I will go and get booze. There's no doubt about it.

I don't have much choice; the thought, it's already planted in the back of my mind (*planted*—it has roots, this thing, buried deeply in every neural connection in my brain; it's indistinguishable from all the snapping synapses that make me what they make me). As soon as I think it, I get excited about it. I'm horrified down to the bone and I'm excited about it.

I don't have a choice because I think about what's outside these walls concurrently with all these thoughts about feeling good, detoxified, happy, healthy. The walls of my apartment are no match for what's outside of them, and what's outside of them is alcohol. And it's not even alcohol that I'm worried about and that I'm addicted to, exactly. It's my thoughts that are my addiction, the way they start with "I should get some food" and morph into "How about a bottle of wine?"

And my addictive thoughts are not like other thoughts. They are not stoppable; they are never easily distracted. Which is why my addiction is also a body part. I can't get rid of it any easier than I can cut off my own arm or poke my eye out.

———

I pack Frankie's diaper bag. I take my time getting him ready, dressing him in matching shirt and socks, a hat with teddy-bear ears, mittens the size of tulips. He's gurgling and smiling. He knows we're going out, he probably thinks—or whatever it is that he processes in his little brain—that this is about him.

———

I've never been arrested but I always feel guilty whenever a cop or a cop car goes by. Maybe it was the four days in isolation, but when I see the cop car, I'm convinced that somebody tipped them off about what I did the first night: drank a bottle of wine and some vodka while the baby was asleep in his bassinet, completely and pathetically dependent on me and my drunken self. Who's going to believe that I've been sober for the past 3.5 days? I imagine a neighbor, somebody from across the street watching me through binoculars, a telescope, taking notes, taking photos, reporting, reporting.

To serve and protect it reads on the side of the cop car.

Briefly, I have a thought of flagging it down and asking for a ride. My back is killing me. If the cop says no I'll point to the serving part of that slogan. Serve me. Protect me. Protect me from me.

I do no such thing. Frankie and I continue on our walk. I smile at the cop behind the wheel and he doesn't smile back. I didn't expect him to anyway. I wish I had the guts to ask him to arrest me.

———

I have some sense left with me because when I get to the liquor store I suddenly remember the light beer that I used to drink in the summer and so I only get a six-pack of that. In the evening, after putting Frankie to bed, I smoke a pack of cigarettes and I try to sip—not gulp!—and it's a miracle but I go to sleep almost completely sober with two cans left in the fridge. It is like wrapping an amputation in bandages, but at least I've stopped the bleeding.

AT THE DOCTOR'S

When my boyfriend gets back I am relieved and scared. I'm scared because I know for sure that something is wrong with me. After my week alone and my painful sober sipping, I am so tired of myself and of my own tricks that I feel a need to confess. But I don't know how.

I call my sister to ask her to come over. I'm hoping that her presence will help me get out what I need to get out.

My sister comes over to have dinner with us. As soon as I see her I know that I'll be able to talk. We have a strange relationship where our roles often get reversed—right now, I'm the immature screw-up and she is the wise one even though she is much younger than me.

And so, finally, in a bout of near-sobriety, I tell my sister and my boyfriend that I think I may have a problem with drinking. Again, I mean.

It is no news to them, as it turns out. It's almost as if they were waiting for me to say something because it is immediately decided that I will tell my family doctor about my relapse. I agree with the intervention team that this is a smart idea.

The harm reduction group was nice, my boyfriend says, but it didn't really work out and you clearly need more.

I know.

So you should tell your doctor. See if she has other suggestions.

I will. Because I'm not going back to AA, I say to them.

I know that. I don't want you to go back. You were miserable.

My sister says nothing, but later, she gives me a surprisingly strong hug before she leaves, and I almost cry.

———

At the doctor's, it feels nice to be able to talk to someone who's never heard about my alcohol troubles before. There are no people left in my life who haven't been, at some point, treated to my coming out as a sober alcoholic, years ago, but there are a lot of friends who haven't been aware of my recent relapse.

When I first got sober, there were lots of people in my life who might've wondered if they, too, were alcoholics. My coming out and sobriety were slightly threatening, perhaps—I looked so okay on the outside. The stories of my drinking weren't any wackier than anybody else's. But I lost a few friends over my non-drinking.

In my sobriety, I've made new friends. Those friends, they never knew of the old me snorting mysterious white powder I found on the bathroom floor in a fetish club. Or about burning a hole in an already-infected burned hole in my leg with a cigarette. Or about coming to, naked, with someone's hand around my neck. I didn't share those stories. So my relapse is a big secret, something that I haven't disclosed to any of my new friends because of my shame that it happened.

I wonder if my doctor ever did anything like that—like drinking. Has she ever worried about any weird behavior she engaged in? Did she perhaps go through a tranquilizer stage back in medical school? Morphine? Amphetamines? In medical school, was there an anesthesiologist friend who would organize clinical-death sessions so that people could experience the afterlife, and was she a member of that club?

But there is no way to tell if my doctor has a dark story. She's so organized. She has not misplaced my files, ever. Her pretty blouses and pretty hair are always neatly ironed or draped perfectly over her slim body; she smiles a lot. I've never seen her in green scrubs.

———

She asks me how often.

How often do I drink?

Yes. Every day? A couple times a week?

What is a reasonable amount? I don't say this out loud. I don't drink every day. Every other day. Well, no more than six days a week.

I lie: Maybe once a week.

How many drinks?

Maybe two.

Two?

Two or three.

So two or three?

Sometimes three. But usually two. Two glasses of wine. Sometimes two beers.

She writes it all down. Looks up. Three?

Three at the most.

How are you doing? How are things with your boyfriend?

Okay lately, I say, and consider now my almost sober week when the boyfriend was away. Okay.

And before that? How are things with you in general?

In general, I am exhausted. Running on a few hours of sleep, I spend my days always trying to stay out of the house, walking end-lessly or, alternatively, hogging coffee-shop spaces with my stroller caravan for hours.

I spend money, too, eating ridiculously expensive lunches in res-taurants with a metal-and-glass aesthetic, or shopping. I buy lots of stupid shit I don't need. Like fake eyelashes or decorative masks. Wigs and authentic pointe shoes.

I carry the stroller into subway stations, push it through walk-ing crowds.

I change the baby's diapers on dozens of bathroom floors, breast-feed on top of recycled cardboard.

I stay out because I can't stay in one place. Because I'm running away and because I'm chasing something too.

At the end of every day, I walk into liquor stores and pick some-thing up for later on, after the baby is asleep, and after the formula is prepared for his nightly feeding.

I feel safer at night. Even though at night is when I drink. At night, I am home.

Most nights I stay up watching TV. Most nights I drink while watching TV. Some nights it just seems as if I am not there at all. I am somewhere on the bottom of a lake and my boyfriend's face is barely visible above the surface, maybe calling my name, maybe telling me that he hates me.

Not so good, I tell the doctor. But we're managing.

Does he know you drink?

He does. He was the one who told me to tell you.

Is there alcohol in the house?

There is.

You have to get rid of it. Alcoholism is a family disease, she recites.

It is?

Of course.

I promise my doctor that I will tell the boyfriend to get rid of it. I also promise that I will see Bobby, the social worker at the clinic, to talk to him about my struggles.

———

A realization comes over me: My problem is barely *my* problem now—there are more and more people getting involved and we're all going to make me stop drinking.

I stand up. It is time to go.

———

In my head, a map of the nearest intersection pops right up. I quickly zoom out and move above the clinic. If right now I am at point A on the map, the clinic, there are two destination points, B and C, nearby. The one closer to me is about five hundred meters away from where I am standing. B for the beer store.

It is the one farther west, C, the liquor store, that interests me. A good twenty-minute walk, but it is on the way home.

Immediately, D and E also light up on my imaginary map: two

other liquor stores I could pass walking the same route. There is a whole alphabet in my head, ready to be activated at all times.

————

Are you okay?

Sorry? Yes, yes. Well, I will be.

I know you will, she says. She gives me a gentle smile. Don't beat yourself up about any of it, okay? You should hear from Bobby this week. He's a really great guy, you'll love him. Please give Frankie a big hug from me.

She is the one who delivered my son. A photograph of him sleeping is taped to a corkboard behind her, and beside it she pinned a thank-you card I gave her. The card reads "You're a lifesaver," and it has a picture of a half-drowned pink-eyed mouse inside a life belt.

I wish her a good weekend and leave.

I walk home. I stop at point C and get something for later on.

BETTER NOW

A popular adage going around the rooms of Alcoholic Anonymous was Albert Einstein's "Insanity is doing the same thing over and over and expecting different results."

An alcoholic who is in the throes of addiction believes that the next time she drinks she will be able to drink just enough and no more to find that perfect balance of being buzzed but not falling on her face. And in order to find that ultimate happy spot, an addict will drink just enough—just one more—to perfect that balance. She is almost there, in fact. Perhaps one more drink will add a nice polish to it all, make it just so. At the same time, it's probably a good idea to have one extra drink to ensure this buzz lasts longer. Just in case.

And the morning after is exactly the same as the morning after the last time: full of anxiety, fear, shame, confusion. And the morning promises to self are exactly the same as the last time: I will never do this again.

And in the afternoon, the insanity quietly suggests: Perhaps tonight it will be different. Perhaps tonight you can just have a couple of casual drinks, just get a nice buzz on, don't need to get so drunk.

What a great idea. Let me try that.

Motherhood is a type of insanity, my friend Mary said once. It is not insanity as defined by Einstein because doing the same thing over and over yields different results eventually. In fact, motherhood is based on doing the same thing over and over and getting different results.

Say "Mama."

Nothing.

Say "Mama."

Nothing.

Say "Mama."

Nothing.

Say "Mama."

Nothing.

Say "Mama."

"Mama."

The insanity of motherhood lies in perseveration. You can be all like: "I'm going to count to three!" . . . but there's always three and three-quarters.

You will read the same five storybooks tomorrow before bed.

There's never a last time you'll forgive your child for biting you. You need to make the dinner tomorrow again.

Just when you want to abandon doing the same thing over and

over again, you need to do it one more time. Motherhood is an infinity of second chances. It is insanity by repetition.

———

It gets cooler outside and I'm still restless.

Staying in is out of the question, as the boyfriend works from home.

In the beginning, we both tried to pretend that he's not here—after all, I am the one getting paid for being on mat leave—but we failed. I felt overwhelmed, asking him to help me with the baby, him saying he's not home—saying to consider him *not-home*—and we'd end up getting ridiculous with each other, threw tantrums like children: He'd pack his laptop bag with fury, say he's going to leave, I'd say not to bother, I'm leaving, it's fine. I'd drop everything on the ground as I'd try to get ready with shaky, angry hands before flying out the door. I'd slam the door.

This happened a few times too many, so to avoid further conflicts, I end up on long outings with the stroller every day. It's getting cold, but I bundle up, pack a big bag of diapers, and I'm off. I bring my laptop with me and write stories in coffee shops all over the city as the baby naps.

I also try to get back into one of my old hobbies, photography. In the beginning, I take many pictures of myself, but I quickly run out of patience for myself. I have nothing to say with these self-portraits.

Which is why I contact some friends who like to model; post a couple of casting calls online, on the amateur-model site. There are always some musicians or some actors who need pictures and who are willing to model for free in exchange for the photos. It's the perfect deal.

I start daydreaming about doing this for a living. Perhaps I won't go back to my job but work as a freelance photographer instead. How cool would that be?

———

One of the first models I photograph is Chris. She's a talented musician I know from before, when I used to be sober and she used to be drunk. She's putting out an album and needs some artwork done for it.

When I meet her I can't tell if she's drinking or not, but her thinness impresses and worries me. Her legs are like sticks in boots. She shakes and twitches in the cold. She composes herself and stays still or jumps in perfect half arches when I snap pictures. She goes back to shaking and twitching in between.

She looks fantastic in almost every frame. Her eyes are green and sick-looking, too big. She wears a scarf that is twenty meters long, or it seems that way; it is a very long scarf.

The baby is asleep in the stroller, tucked inside his warm onesie under layers of blankets. This is the time of long baby sleeps. He's growing rapidly, his body full of rolls and dips and cheeks. Dimpled bum and double chins.

———

When we're done taking pictures, I tell Chris I will walk her to her bus stop.

I should probably just go home. It's close to five; I could go home. I have a whole camera card full of photographs I can work on. I love working on photographs.

But I don't go home to do what I love.

I want to walk Chris to her bus stop at the bottom of the hill.

We walk and talk about the place where we met five years ago, in "the rooms." Neither of us has gone back; we both say we don't need to. Her sister is worried about her, Chris says, but there is nothing to be worried about.

My sister is worried about me, I say, and we laugh.

My mother is on my case too, Chris says.

I think to myself how embarrassing it is that I didn't know she had a sister and a mother. Suddenly, there are people I have to add to my knowledge of Chris—a sister, a mother—who worry about her, tell her to get her act together. There are normal, regular-people parts in Chris's life. She isn't just an orphaned rock star who smokes too much rock when she goes on a bender.

She says her sister is kind of square.

Compared to Chris a lot of people are kind of square so I don't really get any idea what her sister is like thanks to this description.

My sister is square too, I say, and Chris nods.

But what's with all this sister and mother fussing-about? How is Chris doing now anyway, really?

Really? She's doing fine and, honestly? It's just a question of self-discipline. Just a way of thinking and being responsible for yourself.

I say I know what she's talking about. I, too, am self-disciplined enough to manage on my own.

I wonder if Chris is lying to me.

More important: Did she notice that we had just walked by a sign pointing to a liquor store?

Will she go back to the liquor store once I leave her at the bus stop?

It's a small sign. You wouldn't notice it unless you looked for it, or unless your brain is trained to spot signs like that. And there is no way of knowing that there is a liquor store in the building to our right, unless, of course, you know that there is a liquor store there. It is a new liquor store, but if you don't live around here how would you know?

Chris doesn't live around here. She lives in Kensington Market. There is one liquor store near the market. I don't live there but I know about it, the one with the big handicapped elevator.

At the bus stop, we hug. Promise to keep in touch.

———

I push the stroller back up the hill, the building with the liquor store now to my left. I walk slowly. The baby is sleeping. The camera is bouncing against my hip so I bend down to shove it in the basket underneath the stroller.

I walk to the top of the hill. I turn left.

In front of the liquor store I think about Chris. What if she was honest? If someone like Chris is staying sober and managing, Chris, a rock-star crackhead who I heard used to be homeless, why can't I? How bad am I that I can't do what Chris is doing to stay sober?

Or is Chris waiting for me to go away, at the bottom of the hill, letting the bus drive off? Waiting so that she can go to the liquor store herself?

———

I stand in front of the store for some time.

I never stand in front of the store, I just go in—as if diving off a board.

But this time I stand in front of the store and I wait. First, I wait for Chris to show up. Then I wait not to go in.

I get tired standing in front of the store, so I sit on a concrete tree planter. People go in and out of the store.

I let my mind go while I sit there and wait for nothing. My mind flies all over the place, but mostly it swirls around the box or the bottle.

I've already decided to go in.

No, the decision was made for me; it was always there in the back of my mind. I was lying to myself about waiting for the decision to go away or change its course.

There is a sudden acceptance: I am going to go in anyway, always, because I have no choice. There are no decisions; the action will be prompted by an involuntary muscle, a breath going in and out; it is a natural process for me.

I get up and go in.

———

The relief once I leave the store, my fix on the bottom of the stroller hidden in the camera bag? Unreal. This is true happiness.

It is as if someone suddenly adjusted focus on the world around me, added an extra bounce to my walk, sang a sexy song to my hips, made me giddy with anticipation.

Should I get another one?

———

Chris's not showing up at the liquor store, and probably just taking the bus and going home, is the one thought that bothers me that evening while I am still able to talk back to my thoughts.

ON THE GO

My drink choices, they change, but vodka remains a staple. I believe it to have the least amount of odor. It looks clear, it smells pretty straightforward—it can't possibly be that difficult to mask, can it? I do sometimes smell it coming from my pores, though. Unlike Scotch or beer, vodka seems too clean to leave a stink on the body. It often does, though, and then I have to invent stories about spoiled perfume and smoke like crazy all the time to stink up the stink.

———

My ritual is to buy my alcohol near the end of my daily walk with my son. It's getting colder and colder outside; winter is almost here now. This new degree of cold is wet, penetrating. I look inside the stroller. The baby's blue hat inside the hoodie of his snowsuit barely fits him at all now, and the pompom is missing. His cheeks are bright red, scary red. I have to go somewhere inside to wait it out, this cold. It's dinnertime, we should be eating dinner. Normal people eat dinner now. But I'm not normal, nothing is normal. I have an urge.

I get dizzy as soon as I think about it. And I think about it all the time. I have an urge. No, not an urge, it's not an urge. It's a calling. An order from the sky or from the ground below me, or from the air around me, who knows.

It propels me and then everything feels like free fall. It can be stopped only one way.

I'm pushing the stroller but I want to abandon the stupid thing and start running.

I'm chasing the feeling of wanting to get high and I'm running away from it.

———

The urge has been planted even earlier. The urge is a plant and the seed has landed earlier in the day, or earlier in the month or in the year, or in my genetic makeup. It has forced itself into the deepest consciousness. It was the fastest-growing plant on my planet and now it's a baobab, indestructible, strong and veiny with my own blood powering its roots. I'm overpowered by this plant—it crushes my insides with its insistent branches. Eventually, there's no room for my insides, for my lungs. Which is why I breathe faster—I hear it, too, it's louder, my breath—to make the breath last longer. I feel my body sweat. The good thing is that now I'm warmer. I'm no longer freezing, just wet and hot and crazy. I speed up. A map in my head indicates that there's one close by.

Finally, I see what I've been looking for. I slow down. The world seems to slow down too. It's as if we are in a film, getting to the climax, the part where the heroine arrives at the fountain of youth or whatever she's after.

Yes. I'm here. I've arrived.

It will be nice and yellow and light inside. It will be warm. There will be rows and rows of colors. Beautiful ambers and crystal whites and tropical blues and deep, blood-pulsing reds. There will be golden plaques with impressive numbers stamped on them, and new-born flirty labels on wines, with names like *Ladies Night Out* that appeal to women, and *Fat Bastard* for men. There will be so much glass, a symphony of glass. I can't wait to hear it.

———

The door opens soundlessly and we're inside this wonderland. Frankie is awake and he scans the rows of colors and crystal with his big eyes. I'm sure it's interesting, all the colors. His mouth is open as he looks and looks. He babbles quietly, under his breath. His head is turning left and right.

I don't go to this particular liquor store often so I let myself relax and peruse the shelves a little bit. In my usual liquor stores I make this a quick in-and-out because of the guilt. I'm just being paranoid but I think that people remember me. I think that people tend to remember the that-doesn't-belong-here thing: the stroller.

I explore a little. I'm always amazed by all the new alcohol that has come out since I got sober. I check out the new diet beers and Scotches and vintage wines that share a birthday with me.

And vodkas!

All these flavored vodkas: orange, tangerine, grapefruit, raspberry, strawberry, blueberry, vanilla, blackcurrant, chili pepper, cherry, apple, cinnamon, cranberry, peach, pear, passion fruit, pomegranate, plum, mango, white grape, banana, pineapple, coconut, mint, melon, rose, buffalo grass.

I go for the plain. Vodka-flavored vodka.

At the cash register, Frankie smiles at the store clerk and I feel paranoid again, paranoid enough to mumble something about having a party. She coos to Frankie and nods to me while giving me the correct change. I want her to scream that she should report me to Children's Services or something, but, really, I don't want her to even notice that I'm here.

––––

Around the same time, in the fall, I move my drinking times counterclockwise. I occasionally drink when it's still light out. I suppose I miss summer. I miss its light and the carelessness of it, the bike rides, the way you can just throw out a bottle without worrying about wet fingers getting stuck in the freezing cold metal mouths of garbage bins. It is perhaps because I miss summer that I go on a sparkling-wine kick. It's also because I still have it in me to pretend that I'm not drinking things like straight vodka on a regular basis that I decide I should drink sparkling wine in order to slow down a bit. It tastes better than beer, it has a low alcohol content—but not too low—and it smells kind of like juice. I also imagine that it will put me in just the right mood—not too sloppy and not too blacked-out. It will put me in the champagne mood, which is where I would like to be at all times. It will put me right back in the summer.

––––

The popping cork is, of course, a problem. And the bottles are big, thick and clunky. I bring them home, but I'm so nervous about being caught. Early on, a bottle is discovered on the deck, by the boyfriend, and he brings it wordlessly to me, as if it was a baby I had abandoned on the deck; his eyes are that serious.

Why were you on the deck, were you snooping around? I shout.

He doesn't shout. I'm the shouter in the family. We are a family.

Snooping for what? He tells me to calm down. He says I will wake the baby. I calm down. Then I make up some lie about how the bottle must be left over from an a deck party—maybe when Frankie was born and all those people were coming over with booze—and he pretends to believe me.

———

After that one bottle is found, I drink my sparkling wine away from the house. I develop a new ritual.

My ritual involves going to the grocery store first to get formula, followed by a visit to the liquor store to get sparkly, and then getting a bottle of Sprite in a convenience store. Next, I march to the nearest grocery store or coffee shop and lock myself in the bathroom. I have the perfect excuse too for staying in there for a long time: I always ask about a changing table.

In the bathroom, I first fill a couple of baby bottles with formula. Next, I empty the bottle of Sprite into the sink. Then I gently tap the cork of the sparkling wine and twist it while holding it. It always makes the loud, hollow popping sound, of course, but nothing so crazy you'd have to make up stories. I usually remember to flush the toilet at the same time, just in case.

What a loud shit I just had.

The baby is fascinated by what's going on—all those purposeful movements, the opening of formula cans, the popping of the bottle, and liquids being poured in, out and in while I talk to him.

I tell him that he's a very, very good baby. This is all for you, baby, I say and I go on with my performance until the bottle of Sprite is filled up again. We can go now, I announce, and we go.

I imagine a pimply-faced teenage grocery store employee discovering the empty formula cans, the bottle of Prosecco in the trash, forced to suddenly think all kinds of suspicious, troubling thoughts about her boss.

After the bathroom I can go for a nice final walk in the cold, taking big sips out of my Sprite with stiff, freezing lips until I'm ready to go home and do whatever I do there. If it gets too cold I smuggle it into a coffee shop. In the chaos of strollers, coats, hats and boots, nobody ever notices the little sips.

———

People wandering around like me—are they, too, locking themselves in the bathroom, mixing their concoctions? Are they looking to discreetly throw out their empties? Are they hiding things in the linings of their purses and strollers and coats?

Can they tell I do it too?

How could you tell?

Because if you were to look at the evidence tape you'd see me and I look nothing like a drunk. I look good. In fact, if you'd known me before I relapsed, you might even think that I seem better than ever, and that motherhood serves me really well. Example? I've lost some weight. You can see my cheekbones.

Still, I keep looking for cues in others. When I'm out on my walks, I watch other moms. The city is filled with them, rain or shine—the days belong to new moms. We are an army of stroller pushers. We all push equally—the healthy-looking yoga ones and the ones who are like rock stars with tattoos and lipstick, the butchy ones, and the ones who, like me, treat these daily outings seriously and dress up for the occasion in fur vests, killer dresses and hats. And I just know that many of them are carrying empties in their diaper bags. And some of them are walking around with open cans of beer or sparkly wine mixed with Sprite secured in the stroller's cupholder. Or they're cooing to babies in coffee shops while taking discreet sips out of their bottles of Sprite.

Right?

I look in their faces and a lot of them smile back the way first-time moms do to one another when we recognize our common plight, new children and all the pushing.

I look for signs of secrets, but I can't read anything into all these smiling stranger faces.

And this makes me feel as though I'm the only one. This makes me feel so alone. And so superior the way a secret makes you feel, even if it's a bad secret, even if it's killing you.

I stop and take a big sip from my bottle of Sprite to calm my nerves.

NEW HOME

Besides drinking and thinking about how lonely I am, I devote my free time to further self-care. The baby is still sleeping a lot, and I try to keep busy so I don't drink too much during the day now that I've begun that scary phase. For now, I manage to count between drinks and never go beyond my limit. I'm a day sipper, an evening drinker. I'm a night drunk.

To kill the time that stretches between my drinking rituals, I get regular haircuts and facials. I shop. Being a mother now, I finally feel entitled to small luxuries. I buy my first fur, first Marc Jacobs.

I tell myself this is because I deserve it. I had the Pain. Twenty-three hours of it and eighteen staples in my stomach to prove I've earned my place in the pantheon of being a grown-up. I'm a grown-up. I'm just like the other mothers I pass.

But it's not about being a mother. And of course, I've decided, I'm nothing like the other mothers because of my awful secret.

The truth?

This is not about deserving some luxuries. It is not about being a grown-up at all. But it is with the grown-up stuff that I'm covering the rot. Underneath all this dress-up I'm falling apart. I'm gluing together all the pieces that are falling off with all that nail polish and fur and other crap. Nothing stays put. Even though it looks put.

———

There are less gracious looks, like the one in the middle of a snowstorm, one of those dark winter months, December, that doesn't want to ever go away.

Again, me with the stroller. The baby inside it, warm and cozy in the blankets. Me with a lost glove, frozen right hand clutching a can, big Sorels with laces wrapped around the ankles, winter jacket flopping open: this late at night, I don't feel cold anymore. I'm fine. I sing. I walk.

———

I forget how I got to nightfall because I left the house relatively early. After I left the liquor store, I had lunch at some bar. It was still light outside. And when we came out of the bar, the sun was still hitting the snow, making everything look like an overexposed photograph.

How is it that it is suddenly late and I'm woozy with drunkenness?

———

The baby wakes up and I coo to him. I love you so, so much, I tell him. You're awesome. He is just so awesome. You're the awesomest baby in the world, I say to him.

I want to eat him. Instead, I find a bottle of formula and stick it in his wet, rose-red mouth. He sucks on the bottle energetically, his huge brown eyes—my eyes—roaming all over my face.

I look down at my boots, sloshing through the melting snow, and the remains of the day still sparkling, reflected in all that dirty water around my feet.

My phone rings and rings and when I pick up it's my boyfriend text-messaging me from the new house where he's waiting for us. I don't text him back.

Forward to a random side street.

Now I'm pushing through the snow, which is falling harder and harder. The day is completely gone, and with it all its light. Everything is cooler, quiet, dimmer. But despite the cold, I'm hot in my big drunken Sorel boots.

I open my sweater under my coat. Even better. There's that open tall can of Heineken in my hand too. The streets are empty. I'm singing again. Or maybe the whole time.

I'm singing because I'm really happy. We are walking toward our new house. I've never owned a house before. I don't really own one now but it's the closest I've got to it. My boyfriend owns it and I'm going to be living with him.

This is why I'm happy.

I have a few more cans in the diaper bag, enough to last me until we get to the new house. This is also why I'm happy.

———

The snow is getting bigger, thicker, there's more and more of it, coming down from the sky and blowing at me from the sides. I hear my phone ringing somewhere on the bottom of my purse.

I have to stop singing because it's hard to in this wind, but I remain happy. I'm pushing the stroller through all this windy whiteness, and in my head I count the cans in the diaper bag: There should be four left. With this open one it's four and a half, although more like four and one-third.

Then we are a little bit lost or maybe a little bit closer to our goal. Who can tell? The goal, the new house, is somewhere to our left; we should be turning at some point. The phone rings and I almost answer and consider asking my boyfriend if he could tell me where we are.

It is snowing even more now, so I stop and secure the plastic stroller cover over the stroller. I close it tight to make sure the baby is okay in there, dry and warm.

I have some trouble moving my right hand. It seems to be frozen around the can. I have no way to unbend all the fingers. I'll unbend them later. For now, I stick the hand with the empty can in my coat pocket to warm it up.

The good thing about all this snow is that you can hide things in it so easily. My warmed-up hand lets go, I drop the empty can, kick some white over it; it's gone. Nobody sees it. Nobody is out in this weather. Except for me—the happy woman with the stroller.

———

Eventually, we stop at a laundromat. There's a man inside and he grunts in response to my request to let us sit down and rest. Through the plastic I see that the baby is asleep inside his cozy fish tank on wheels.

It's so thick with snow outside, the street lights look like ghosts.

I buy a ginger ale from a vending machine to appease the laundry man and also to mask the smell. I don't know if it will mask the whole day, but it'll have to do.

I have one more can left in the diaper bag. Only one can? The liquor-store map pops up in my head. We are a good twenty minutes away from the liquor store at the nearby plaza. It's way past eight now. In this snowstorm I won't make it before nine, when the store closes. I'd make it by myself but not with the stroller. Maybe this is a good thing.

I open the Heineken in the diaper bag and the ginger beer simultaneously, to combine the sound. I take a small gulp from the ginger ale can, a huge gulp from the other can. I take my big furry hat off and swoosh my hair around. Next, I loudly bring down the can of pop onto the table so that the laundry man can see that I've no bad intentions and am just taking a little breather here, drinking my pop before I continue on through the snow.

My boyfriend calls again and I answer and in the straightest voice I can manage, give him updates like a correspondent: We've already turned the corner at the main intersection, yes. We are a few blocks away. I believe. We're almost home.

Where are you right now?

Right now? Right now I'm in the laundromat.

He says something, not sure what because the connection is weak, so I hang up. I get up and stick my head out and squint to see the name of the street. It's the name of my street. Our new street.

The phone rings again. It's my boyfriend and he's saying something again, who knows what.

I say I'll see you in five and hang up.

I leave the laundromat.

I take a long, filling gulp from the last can and drop it and kick it into a snowbank. Drunk, I'm a disgusting litterbug.

———

Then we're home.

We're home.

———

Home is a forest of boxes. Our entire lives are packed up inside. It's random: picture frames with pillows and a coat in one box, a set of champagne flutes in a cardboard divider, a squeaky soft toy and my bathing suits in a plastic bag in another.

Did you have a little drinkie tonight? my boyfriend says.

So he can smell it on me after all.

This is our game: He can tell and I can tell that he can tell but I'll say no, and he'll say, No? Are you sure? And I'll say, No, I am sure, even though I know that he knows that I know that he knows.

Are you sure?

I'm sure.

He'll ask one more time, probably. This time, I will bare my teeth. He will back away, Okay, okay. Sorry. Just checking.

Checking what?

Nothing. Forget it. I'm sorry, I'm just high-strung because of the move.

———

The baby is home and safe, but I don't recall when we took him out of the stroller and where we've left him. He could be in one of the boxes, for all I know.

I want to move furniture.

It's late, my boyfriend says.

This house needs more space, I declare.

My boyfriend—I have no idea where he is at this point. He doesn't register. Maybe he's in one of the boxes too, with the baby. No matter. I'm driven by the need for space but mostly by the need for destruction. The need comes on sometimes when I've been drinking too much. I'm usually a quiet drunk—always pretending not to be drunk—but tonight I feel fired-up from all the walking and singing and all that snow.

I discover my dresser buried underneath a pile of boxes. I try to pull it out but it's stuck. Fucking thing.

I'm filled with energy and anger, thawing in the warmth of the house. It's a physical reaction, this rage, but it's also caused by knowing I'm this drunk. Right now I'm extra-disappointed in myself. The disappointment is constant and I get drunk because of the constant disappointment, but usually I am quiet about it. Not tonight. Tonight I am so disappointed I can barely see.

I kick the dresser and something gives, a leg buckles down or something. The whole thing is suddenly sitting legless, on the floor, and it's puking up drawers.

Fucking ridiculous thing.

My boyfriend's voice says to leave it alone, we'll deal with it tomorrow. The baby must be upstairs because I hear his thin wail somewhere above me and I scream, My baby, as if someone was murdering him—and someone is, possibly—and I plough through the boxes to rescue him. My boyfriend follows me up the stairs because he probably knows what I know: that he knows.

The baby is fine, sleeping, quiet.

Just a nightmare, I tell my boyfriend, and he nods, knowingly.

Let's just go to sleep, he says, and I almost agree but then I remember: the dresser.

The disappointment comes up again.

I explain that if I don't deal with this fucking dresser right now I will explode.

I don't know if my boyfriend hates me right now but just in case he doesn't, I've got enough disappointment to make up for it.

He lets me deal with the dresser. Or do whatever. He goes to sleep or something. He disappears, again, along with the dresser and the boxes and the baby, in the vortex of my blackout.

———

There's one flashback of me dragging the dresser on the sidewalk, away from our new house. The drawers are in it, I think; in this flashback I see myself pushing them back inside the dresser's mouth once, twice, again. The dresser is a bomb about to detonate. I drag it far, in the snowstorm, drag it to the end of the street—white falling, then it's dark again.

———

In the morning, on my way to the convenience store, I see the dresser. It's sitting right on the corner of our street. Its top is covered in a thin layer of new snow. The drawers are gone. I wonder if I took them out or if someone else did.

I say nothing about the dresser or the missing drawers as my boyfriend and I walk by it later on that evening. He says nothing about it. I have no way of guessing the level of his own disappointment.

AT THE COUNSELOR'S

Shortly after our move, my doctor's office calls to remind me about an appointment with a counselor. I don't remember making this appointment, but every time I pile up clean underwear on the carpet in the corner of my bedroom I remember the dresser. The lack of the dresser suggests in its symbolic way that I probably could use another person to talk to.

The counselor, Bobby, has patterned green socks. Everything about him suggests gentleness, but the subtle flamboyance of his socks makes me a little suspicious. I know it's crazy, but his socks make me distrust him.

I have Frankie with me. He's stirring in the stroller. Bobby mentions a grown daughter. He asks me the standard questions.

I give him the standard lie: divide amounts and days by two, then divide them by two again.

Bobby's voice is so soft it almost lulls me to sleep. It at least puts me into some kind of a semi-coma because later I can't remember anything that we talked about, only those damned socks and how close his office is to point C on my mental map.

———

In our second session, a week or so later, Bobby suggests that I may be depressed or suffering from anxiety and maybe this is why I drink and why I suffered from an eating disorder in my twenties: an old demon I had mentioned to my doctor a long time ago that is documented in my chart.

I dislike the words *suffering*, *suffered*. As if I had done something heroic like my grandma, getting captured by the Nazis and sent to a work camp and surviving. I never heard her use those words. But okay, *suffered*. Suffering.

I nod.

Bobby waits with a tranquil smile.

Well, I am very, very anxious, I say. All the time. I used to take Ativan. It really works for me. Can you talk to my doctor about it? My hands tingle and freeze and half of my face spasms from anxiety. Feels like I'm always sitting on the edge of my seat, figuratively and literally, you see, because anxious people like me, they can never sit still so they sit on edges. I'm definitely. Suffering from anxiety.

Bobby nods a lot at this and stops to write things down.

Today his socks are pink, purple, orange.

There's a drawing of a sailing ship on the wall. Light pastel colors; even the blue looks more like yellow, that's how mellow it is. Bobby's socks are the brightest objects in the room.

I would love to know what he's writing down. Grocery list like all shrinks, probably.

I wait for him to finish.

Frankie makes a noise in his sleep. He's with me again.

Bobby blinks friendlily, Do you always take care of the baby?

I'm the baby manager, I say.

A "baby manager"—that's funny, Bobby says softly in his singsong voice and scribbles again.

(Tomatoes. 2 lb brown sugar. ~~Bok choy.~~ Rapini?)

He says, So. Not enough time for Jowita. What does Jowita like to do?

This throws me off. Jowita. Who the hell knows what she likes to do. I don't know. I like to write and watch TV. And take photographs. And, before, I liked sex. I liked dressing up for parties. And flirting. I guess. Ask me what I love, that's easier. I'm certain about what I love. I love, love, love drinking. Being drunk.

To Bobby I only say the part about photography, and this seems to satisfy him because he writes things down again. He must have at least a month of grocery shopping planned by now.

I say, So. What should I do? Since photography doesn't seem to be working.

We exchange a couple of polite blinks. As we do, I hope and pray and beg every god that I can think of that he will say he's going to talk to my doctor about prescribing me something, some Ativan, some other miracle magical medicine like that. Instead Bobby says, There are special programs for artists to deal with issues like anxiety. We have a great program here at Western, it's through our artist clinic. Let me look it up quickly.

He half turns to his computer to look it up quickly.

―――

I took a program like that some years ago. It was called Mindful Meditation and it was full of misfits like me: a woman who was socially anxious; somebody who stopped talking after a serious car accident, out of fear of losing her voice; a bunch of chronic dieters; a shitload of actors and actresses. We sat in the circle and discussed feeling feelings. One time we spent most of the session learning to meditate while eating, and we chewed on a piece of raisin for minutes, talking about it and feeling feelings afterwards. Near the end of each session we lay on mats and meditated. I always fell asleep, which was an okay thing to do. Eventually, I chose to stay at home and sleep there instead.

―――

I wonder what Bobby looks like naked. I don't want to see him naked but I wonder what he looks like naked. Or what he looks like when he's having sex.

He probably leaves his socks on.

―――

Frankie opens his eyes. His mouth turns downward, but before he has a chance to wail, I pull him out of the stroller. On my lap he's already making a sucking sound, eyes closing in bliss the way they do when he's feeding. Bobby swivels in his chair.

I reach inside my shirt, say, Do you mind?

Of course not.

With Frankie at my breast I feel like a double human. Superhuman. Superior to this twit with his twitty socks and his language of suffering and his feeling feelings programs.

Frankie starts sucking.

I can't do that program, I say. It doesn't work for me.

Okay.

Okay.

What about going to an inpatient treatment?

What about it? Like rehab?

Yes. Have you thought about going away to a treatment center? Bobby turns around, toward his computer again. He says, I'm printing a couple of pages anyway for you to take when you leave. There's a lot of useful information about some in-treatments.

The printer in the corner of the office starts choking and then spits up pages.

Sure, I say.

Frankie's head jerks back at the exact same moment Bobby turns to face me with the printed pages in his hand. My nipple, erect, pink and shiny with milk, pokes proudly out of my shirt. I try to move Frankie's head back onto it immediately, but he jerks back even more violently and starts wailing. I don't look at Bobby.

I'm so sorry, I say.

Oh, it's okay.

I stuff my breast into my shirt, push down on it to hide it further— I'm suddenly annoyed with myself and not superhuman at all—and Frankie, seeing this new development, turns up the screaming volume. I take out my other breast, as discreetly as I can, flip the baby around on my lap and press him against the nipple.

Bobby gives me the same tranquil smile.

———

Outside, it's winter still but I'm sweating like crazy, from all the breastfeeding exercises and everything else that went on in Bobby's office. I open my jacket as I walk. I don't make a right turn toward the liquor store.

Instead I walk south to the main street where on the corner there's a Native meeting center. I like to walk by this corner. It's sad and thrilling. A proverbial car crash you've got to stop and watch except this one has been happening for ages so people stopped stopping. The corner, it's usually swarmed with street people in various stages of drunkenness.

There are squeegee kids with mohawks and piercings, in military boots. They are always surrounded by mean-looking dogs, pit bulls and pit bull crosses and other four-legged jerks.

Besides the kids, there are some older people, shiny and mauve in the face, with dirty, stringy hair. The genders in both groups are almost impossible to discern. There's lots of hugging and cursing. There are big plastic bottles of beer or wine or Listerine going around; everyone smokes. There's always some version of a lady in a robe and slippers, with a gray and sunken face, sitting and smoking to the side: freshly released.

There's often a guy taking his clothes off, yelling, yelling, yelling. There's a girl, too young to live this way but with front teeth missing already when she smiles at the stroller passing her by. There's almost always a police car.

I'm passing by with the stroller.

And I tell myself to watch them, watch them close.

This is me. This is me passing by with the stroller.

This is me too, watching me passing by.

I'm right here, on this corner.

I'm the lady in the winter parka but with slippers on, with matted hair and unseeing eyes.

I'm the yelling guy.

I'm the guy with the giant plastic bottle of beer, falling asleep with a string of mucus hanging out of his nose, freezing. I'm the kid with a squeegee. I'm the dog with fleas and bared teeth.

MORNING AFTER

I have no idea where I am. Or how. Or when.

My guess is that I've missed the actual kick. Was there a kick? I wake up feeling like a heel is lodged in my solar plexus. It must be my solar plexus because from what I remember about it, this is the body part that, if kicked, draws the breath right out of you. And since I can't breathe and there's tremendous pressure somewhere in the top middle of me, I'm most likely right—it is my solar plexus.

I don't want to open my eyes.

I'm lying on a hard surface. It's not my bed, obviously.

———

I'm lying on the carpet and there's a heel digging right into me and I'm struggling to breathe. I already know that there's no heel digging into me and that I can, in fact, breathe. But I am so terrified that the anxiety is making me hold my breath. It's either this, the breath-holding, or I don't know—I'll die.

How could I die?

I could get up, with my eyes still closed, and just start to run. Depending on where I am I could potentially run into a window, a wall, a mirror. I could fall out this window and break my neck, my head could smack into the wall so perfectly that it would impact just the place where my skull would cave in and kill me, and the mirror could shatter and slice my arteries.

Not to be overdramatic but right now anything seems better than being inside this anxiety.

———

And this is not the first time I have woken up with this type of anxiety, thinking of ways to annihilate myself instead of confronting what could possibly be outside my eyelids. This is the anxiety well known to blackout drunks coming out of the soft, merciful abyss, the dam breaking, the questions rushing in: Where? How? When? Wherehowwhen?

———

The more awake I am, the more I know. For example, I already know that I'm at home. I can hear my boyfriend saying something somewhere in the house. He talks in his cat voice, meaning he's talking to one of the cats. If he's talking, that means he is alive. I didn't kill him. So, that's good.

His voice sounds calm. That probably means that he doesn't know yet that the baby is dead, or he knows and has gone mad.

Or the baby is not dead.

Maybe I didn't kill the baby?

I have to check if the baby's alive.

I open my eyes.

I'm on the floor in the baby's room.

———

I see his crib. Here's his hand. Here's the inside of his elbow, the tiny sleeves. Golden curls spilling out from behind his masterpiece of an ear. Here's his beautiful, chubby-cheeked face. His eyelashes so thick and long they look fake, impossible, but they're real. His mouth a shade of kissed red like a kiss itself. His lovely chin, a perfect bow of a bone.

I look at his red mouth again.

I hold my breath.

He is breathing.

I will never do this again. I promise. Thank you, thank you, thank you. He's breathing.

———

I sit up. I'm wearing my soft yellow robe. Underneath I'm wearing nothing.

I will never do this again. I promise.

What I'm never going to do again I don't know. I don't remember much. I remember being downstairs and watching something on TV. Talking to someone on the phone, laughing very loudly, talking about Bobby, the broken dresser maybe, laughing some more, downplaying, minimizing. My boyfriend making a stupid comment. But what stupid comment? Who cares, it was stupid. He's always getting involved in my business. Did we have a fight?

You don't have to sleep here. Please come to bed, my boyfriend suddenly says somewhere behind me, and the anxiety dissipates a little, and instead of anxious, I'm feeling a tiny bit hopeful.

Before I turn to face him, I try to, madly, quickly—have to be very quick here, like I'm in the military or something—guess what sort of voice he's got there. Is it a mad voice, a sad voice or just a voice? Based on my assessment I'll be able to figure out how to proceed, if there are any mines to avoid, or if we can just call a truce and never in our entire lives talk about what happened last night.

I go for soft. I say, Okay, and wait.

He says quietly, Let's just forget about last night.

I have no idea what he's talking about.

Either way, I ended up sleeping on the floor in my son's room. I've never slept on the floor in his room before. What a loser. I am the opposite of a ghost. My body is here but my spirit is gone.

Come here, my boyfriend says.

I'll call Bobby to see if he can see me tomorrow again.

Today.

Today.

My body follows my boyfriend to our bedroom. It inserts itself under the covers with him. My boyfriend runs his hands over my sore breasts. Even the lightest touch makes them hurt. The baby is getting teeth and my body is what he practices on. My chest is covered in tiny scratches, marks.

My boyfriend is insistent but gentle. He kisses my body all over. He kisses my lips but suddenly moves away from my mouth and says, I can still smell it on you. But he doesn't stop kissing me and touching my body.

My hands touch him back, his skin feels nice. His skin against my skin feels nice. Warm. Except that I'm not really here.

He moves on top of me, spreads my legs open and starts fucking me. His face is buried in my shoulder. I feel the back of his head with my fingers. His hair is short, soft, spiky. I enjoy how it feels. It almost brings me back to my body, how his head feels underneath my fingertips. I try to pull him farther inside me, hold him tighter. I want to feel him. I want to feel something. I consider asking him to choke me. But it's too light outside for that now and I'm almost sober.

———

After the sex, we lie there and I cuddle up to him. I throw my arm across his chest, move as close to him as I can. Smell his cologne. Cedar, musk? I also smell my own hair. Smoky. I can smoke almost a pack a night if I drink. I smoke almost a pack a night almost every night. My boyfriend once said he'd never date anyone who was a vegetarian or who smoked. Then he met me.

I say, I'm sorry, even though I don't exactly know what I'm supposed to be sorry for, but I'm sure there are lots of reasons.

His lips are sexy. They say, You're always sorry.

That's all the sexy lips say.

I lie stiffening now, against his body. I don't know how to reply. He's right. I am always sorry.

I listen to the silence. You can hear it in the house—now that there's a baby, silence, too, has a sound. It sounds threatening. As if something went missing.

He hates me. I hate me.

This thought almost makes me cry. I could say my heart is breaking. But the non-feeling is a bit of an issue with me. I do feel shame and guilt and sometimes anger but beyond that it gets confusing. I understand the idea of sadness but I don't *feel* sad. Still, I feel very guilty, so I think that maybe I could ride on this feeling and maybe some tears will come.

No tears come. Nothing unusual here.

———

I know that the deeper I sink, the more my boyfriend tries to rescue me. He's almost always submerged now, in me, in my drowning. His arms are extending and trying to grasp my body, which is becoming more slippery with every touch. But he needn't try so hard—I am stuck to him, no worries. He couldn't shake me off even if he wanted to. Alcoholics are the worst of the weak. They hang on like leeches, all suction, no spine.

From the bottom of my internal despair some tiny, muddy part of me screams to him that I'm no longer even alive. I scream that I'm drowned, I'm done. I know he'll never hear me screaming from the bottom. He wants to believe there's hope.

He says he forgives me. He says it now. He says, I'll help you.

I wouldn't help me if I were him. But now we have this baby together and I understand why he's saying this, even though it's destroying us.

Thank you.

I try to breathe less noticeably. I am aware that my boyfriend hasn't embraced me back and that my arm just lies there across his chest, like a prop. His eyes are closed.

INTERVENTION

The anxious morning repeats itself more than once, but shortly after my boyfriend's saying he'll help me, he helps me. It's almost Christmas and everyone is in an irritable but clearly generous, helpful spirit.

My sister and my boyfriend tell me to sit down. I don't know why she stayed over but I say nothing about her being here. She came over to be with the baby, my boyfriend says. He couldn't wake me up as usual. The baby wouldn't calm down but he was scared about bringing him to our bed.

That explains it.

Earlier this morning, I found her, my sister, sleeping with the baby, in his office on the camping mattress.

I grabbed the baby and went back to our bedroom.

My boyfriend was just getting up.

I slid back into the bed, hid with the baby, under the blankets. I had no idea what happened. My boyfriend said something but I didn't reply. It was safer to act indignant.

———

By the time they tell me to sit down I'm no longer indignant.

I can't hear exactly what is being said, but it's not angry. Their voices are gentle and worried. The baby gets lulled to sleep on my lap by all this worry and gentleness. I almost get lulled to sleep myself. My sister and my boyfriend say things like "sad" and "serious" and "help" and "get through this as a family."

We will, I say. We will. For sure.

Nothing is said for a long time. Everyone looks out the window.

Finally, the boyfriend says, We think you should go to rehab.

I look at my sister. My sister looks scared. She's got a tiny face, big lemur eyes.

Rehab?

They both nod.

I think of the TV show *Intervention* and I imagine cameras zooming in on my face. I arrange my face to appear neutral, friendly but inscrutable. I don't want the audience to guess right away if I will accept the gift that's being offered to me.

Rehab.

But I think it's a great idea, rehab, and I can't believe it will actually happen. To me. A little nobody: me. Nobody ever gets to go to rehab unless they are on TV or are a celebrity. I don't even own a pair of sweatpants. I make a mental note to go out and buy a pair of sweatpants. And a hoodie. I imagine telling my friends, normal people: "When I went to rehab . . . " A woman I knew, a successful model, was thrown in jail for a night. She often told the story of being put in a cell to sober up, and I remember my insides just searing from envy.

Yes, I will go, I tell my sister and my boyfriend, and the camera pans out.

Unlike on TV, the next scene is not of me in a car on my way to the airport on my way to Pine Lodge or Passages. The next scene is of the baby waking on my lap and turning his mouth upside down and me taking out my small breast, like a floppy old sandwich, and stuffing the breast sandwich in the baby's mouth to shut him up before he starts crying.

HOME FOR THE HOLIDAYS

Someone calls me to remind me about a referral for a rehab and I go to the mental hospital to do another test that tells me I'm in trouble. Then I meet with yet another counselor after the results are in. We talk about my options. She, too, would like me to go away, remove myself from my surroundings; she thinks that would be the best for me.

The place is called New Hope. The program is short, less than a month, but it still seems impossibly long to be away from the baby. I'm suddenly not so sure I should be going to rehab. I'll be fine.

The counselor says, well, just in case, she'll request for me to be put on the waiting list. The next session starts in a couple of weeks and there should be some spaces left. It won't hurt to think about it. That's what she says when I say, again, that I doubt I'll be able to leave the baby for that long. I don't make a joke about my thoughts actually hurting.

———

After I leave her office I go and sit in the waiting room. I have to wait for some of my thoughts to stop hurting before I can leave.

I often do this—sit somewhere with no reason other than trying to rearrange what's going on inside my head. I sit in coffee shops, on park benches, at bus stops with buses going by one after another, occasionally in front of liquor stores and, sometimes, in waiting rooms too, after seeing the specialists, though that usually ends up provoking somebody into trying to help me.

On the wall there's the typical rack, jam-packed with cheerful-looking pamphlets on things like "Is Your Spouse an Addict?" or "Everything You Wanted to Know About Amphetamines But Were Afraid to Ask," and a yellowed-paper treatise, "Barbiturates and Alcohol Abuse."

I sit in one of the wide chairs with the thick gray woollen tapestry that has seen the seventies, and wooden armrests with thousands of fingernails driven into their once-glossy finish. I want to cry.

I squeeze and squeeze my eyes and nothing comes out, not even half a tear.

In the end, out of all this effort, my body finally emits a tiny fart into the chair's spongy essence, letting it mix with all the farts from the past.

———

This is our only chance, my boyfriend says over and over when I tell him about New Hope.

Our chance.

I worry that you'll die. I worry that Frankie will die. I'm being selfish when I say I want you to go. Frankie needs a mother. I'll figure it out with him, this is more important.

I'm not that bad, am I?

You are.

———

I spend the rest of the day shopping for things I don't need, spending money, trying to shut up the nagging voice in my head that says my boyfriend is right. In the evening, I fill out an application for rehab and leave a message at the mental hospital saying that I will go. I will go to the earliest session available. Afterwards, on the deck, I quietly, desperately try to get drunk while my boyfriend and the baby are asleep.

Before I pass out for the night, I remember that it's Christmas in less than two weeks and that I haven't prepared for it. I realize, too, that if I go, my New Hope stay will include New Year's Eve, which makes me extremely unhappy and resentful about not having any more alcohol left tonight to binge on before I have to detox prior to entering the program. I am finally able to squeeze out a few tiny tears, over a sad vision I come up with of myself, alone, in a scrawny hoodie, sitting in a room with bars on windows, raising a cup of grape juice to celebrate the new year.

———

I get a confirmation that I can attend the upcoming session at New Hope. Then, right before Christmas, my boyfriend sees multiple flashes of light that aren't there. We don't know this yet but it's his retina detaching.

This is an emergency like any other: nobody is prepared for it. That is the nature of emergencies.

It's the middle of the night, silent cab ride through the empty streets. Fogged-up green street lights in an unusually warm winter. Then it's waiting rooms, the eerie soundlessness of the middle of the night and the middle of waiting rooms. Sticky juice on green plastic chairs, the linoleum floor leading to doors leading to more doors.

More waiting. Long, anxious waiting for specialists to get back to other specialists to see my boyfriend.

The middle of the night, the middle of the waiting.

My sister at home with the baby.

The specialist finally here, the specialist saying it's a giant retinal tear.

Giant? My throat constricting. My boyfriend calmly telling me I cannot have a freak-out right now—this is not about me.

I remember *this* about myself: I used to be good in emergencies. I can be calm, collected. I am the person people used to ask for directions. I can organize a rescue squad. I can hold your hand and get you through the worst.

It is only afterwards that I crumble.

I only hold my shit for so long. When the sirens are on. Once they turn off, I'm gone.

Right now the sirens are on.

I am sorry, I say and I sit quietly, calmly, absorbing all the explanations.

The specialist leaves.

We'll be okay.

You'll be okay, I tell him.

He cries. He is terrified.

I love you.

He is terrified. He cries.

I don't cry. I don't know how.

I go home to check on the baby.

———

I'm back in the hospital first thing in the morning.

I spend hours in the hospital, in more waiting rooms, with the baby in the sling. My beloved boyfriend may be going blind. I cannot think about it.

I want to ask the surgeon if it's possible to take my eye out and give it to him. I am a failure anyway. I am wasting my beautiful, healthy eyes on looking at labels on bottles, on reading charts online about how long alcohol stays in breast milk. I don't deserve my eyes. Is there a way to make this swap?

Stop freaking out, my boyfriend's voice echoes in my head. This is not about you.

Make yourself useful, I order myself.

When he lies in recovery, I go to get him his favorite Booster Juice. I get lost in the hospital on the way back. A very tired doctor tells me I could take the staircase—it will be faster. He doesn't seem to notice the baby on my hip, my frantic and useless eyes. I thank him and he unlocks the staircase door with a card.

I carry the cardboard tray with the cup via the emergency staircase. I feel special—I was let into the secret passage. This sort of adventure is perfect for my secret-agent ways. I'm walking up flights of stairs, balancing the tray and the baby on my hip, in the sling.

When I get to the right floor the door seems to be locked from the outside.

The baby is stirring.

I am sober. I've been sober for a long time now, long for me at least. I sit on the cold stairs and breastfeed.

The juice cup is sweating. Droplets of water sparkle sickly in the fluorescent light of the staircase.

I hear the door open above me.

I shout to wait for me. I shout that I'm locked in here and that there's an emergency. People come down and somebody takes my tray and we walk through the door and I'm led to the recovery room.

I run into my boyfriend's surgeon and he says that the surgery was successful. I ask him if my boyfriend will be able to see once he recovers.

There's an 80 per cent chance, the surgeon says.

I don't like that. I want more.

Yes, I always *want* more. But right now I really *need* more. Just 20 per cent more.

Anything else? the surgeon says.

No.

———

In the recovery room, my boyfriend is lying on his front, his eye bandaged.

The baby squeals through his sleep.

I hold a straw to my boyfriend's lips.

How are you feeling?

Terrible.

But it's over, it's done. We'll be okay.

Okay.

He is falling asleep. He is exhausted, in pain.

This is not fair, I think.

I am so sorry, my love, I think and say nothing.

I am sorry for too much to be able to contain it in one sorry. I am sorry for everything.

———

Later, at home, I call the rehab place and explain to a tired-sounding woman that I have to cancel this term after all.

It's a family emergency, I say, and I know she doesn't buy it. People probably call her with excuses like this all the time.

You have to believe me, I tell her.

Okay.

I really want to go, I lie.

She says, Of course. No problem. These things happen. The next term is in March or June, she says. Could you make either one? The March term falls on Easter.

I'm not religious, it's not why I can't make it this time around, I insist.

Of course.

———

I worry that by March my son will be dead.

I worry that by March I will finally, drunkenly, climb the steep stairs to go to his room to pick him up to kiss him and carry him around, but instead I will, finally, stumble and slip and slide all the way down, with his head bouncing off the steps like a wet deflating ball full of blood. I'll wake up on the carpet afraid to open my eyes again. This time it will be better that I don't open them.

Is there anything earlier than March?

That's the earliest. After that it's June.

In June Frankie turns one. There's no way we'll live to see it if I sign up for June.

March, please. And if there's anything earlier—

There isn't. Sorry.

Well, I'm not ready to quit drinking anyway, I think to myself, trying to forget all the other morbid thoughts.

The woman on the phone reminds me that New Hope is a non-smoking facility and asks if I need to go to a detox before showing up. I'll have to make sure to get myself in at least a week early. They may test me. She says, You don't want to get turned away right at the door, you see. So it's better to detox before.

I don't need to go to a detox, I say as sternly as I can.

The option is there.

No. No detox.

A memory pops into my head. It is one of unmade beds, blank walls, and between the walls dozens of dazed women with matted hair and matted skin. This mixed with the smell of unwashed bodies and tears, candy and tobacco. In the past, as part of practicing my own recovery, I used to go to these places with the message of sobriety. In the past, I was better than detox. I'm not better than detox now but I am stubborn.

The woman on the phone says someone will call me in the beginning of March to do my official intake.

Fine.

She says, I think that's all, unless there's anything else? Good luck with everything at home.

I want to shout that she better be sincere about that because I'm no liar and I really, really need the good luck.

———

When I'm done talking to the rehab woman, I lift the baby out of his crib, get him changed and shoved into his snowsuit. I go to a liquor store and buy bottles of wine and vodka. For the first time in months I don't have to hide any of it. My boyfriend is not allowed to move.

In a last, goodwill effort I call up friends and let everyone know to come over and help.

People show up with food and audiobooks and they sit and talk to us, my boyfriend immobilized on the couch. He has to move as little as possible for the next two weeks. There is a gas bubble in his eye that's supposed to help reattach his retina.

My sister shows up frequently to help with the baby.

I keep the booze outside and get obliterated night after night after a whole day of taking care of the sick boyfriend and the baby.

I'm horrified by my actions.

I am so sorry.

I am pathetically sorry.

If the house is on fire, well, it'll just have to burn.

———

On Christmas Eve, we take some photos. Baby's first Christmas. In the photos, my grin is the biggest and my boyfriend looks terrified. His right eye is covered with a black patch. The eye recovery is going well even though he'll never regain full sight in this eye.

In the pictures, he looks like a pirate in a suit. He is extremely handsome despite or maybe because of the patch. Despite looking terrified. I am not terrified. I am faking being cheerful. Or maybe I am cheerful. I have no idea. I don't know what I am anymore.

My sister's mouth is smiling but not really—it is a tight little smile as if she were trying to eat her lower lip. I can tell from this look that she knows I'm drunk. New Year's Eve is a sad blur of screams and unfinished dinner. I have no idea how this year ends and the next one begins. I black out.

RESEARCH

To prepare for rehab, I watch the TV show about addiction, *Intervention*. I watch it night after night, on my computer—while I drink.

I try to figure something out. I'm not sure what, because it's not the addiction that I try to figure out but the thing that makes people addicts.

I watch lots of episodes. I have seen some before, when I was sober, but now I watch them in a scientific way and I watch them obsessively. I drink and watch. Sometimes I have to rewatch them. That's how it is lately. I rewatch a lot of things.

Maybe I'm so into the show because I want to see that I'm not as bad as most of the people on it. The strung-out junkies bouncing off walls, the alcoholics drinking freely out of jars and jugs and bottles while family members look on helplessly. I'm nothing like the meth addict selling her body for a couple of bucks in front of the 7-Eleven; nothing like the girl who eats pills like candy; not even anything like the estranged mother of three who's in the first stages of cirrhosis of the liver.

I go through Lornas and Joes and Cristys and Aishas. Their faces twist and their eyes scurry around in their sockets like bugs.

———

The more I watch, the closer I feel. To what I don't know, but I know that one more show, one more success story or even a failure, and I'll figure it all out and I will be able to fix myself. I'll get better. At what, again, I'm not so sure, but not moderation because I certainly don't understand the concept of not drinking more once I drink. Once I drink, I miss the stop sign long before I've gone too far.

Perhaps I watch the show because I need to know if there's a way to just stop when I want to, but most important, if there's a way to remain stopped later on in the day.

———

Eventually I even see my own story. I see the effects of immigration, stressed-out parents, small city, big city, big dreams crushed, and I even see people from my own hometown, people who speak my native language.

I never get too close to figuring out how to stop, or what addiction is all about exactly, even though the show's producers always seem to hint at it, at the possible reasons for why it's happened. The counselors on the show refer to addiction as a disease, which only adds to the confusion.

There's always a peak in the story when the subject undergoes something traumatic—death, divorce—or when the ongoing abuse escalates and goes over a certain line. This seems to suggest that there's something—that there is a certain line, for that matter—and that this something is what makes a person into a full-fledged addict. It's as if we're all floating and sometimes gravity brings us down and we touch a soft spot in our lives and when we do, some of us fall right through.

No one is just born an addict, because even the ones with addict parents have siblings who never touch the stuff. And the ones who come from so-called normal families—a minority—seem to be capable of falling into a pile of shit too.

———

Incidentally, everyone, but everyone, is described as having been a happy baby.

———

There's usually a follow-up: close-ups of fattened-up faces, eyes now crystal clear and looking off to the horizon, hair blowing in the wind. Not always.

———

I don't care about reasons that much. I don't buy them. Reasons are arbitrary. My reasons may not be somebody else's reasons.

I keep watching and hoping for some kind of great reveal. But there's no way to predict how each story will end—the keenest reformed druggie might suddenly do a 180 and run off with a bag of crack, the crackiest hopeless case will end working up as a counselor in rehab.

Only one person refuses to go. His episode is one of the last ones

I watch. His name is Adam and he's an alcoholic. I find myself cheering for him when he tells the *Intervention* crew to get lost.

I don't know why but it feels as if he has escaped.

———

After seeing dozens of these shows, after learning nothing and everything about addiction and after Adam destroying whatever I have learned in one powerful fuck-off, I know exactly nothing more about it. And then I finally know one thing—that this is *it* about addiction. You can film it and talk and write about it but there's no way to capture it. It's a black hole. A black hole sucking us—the addicts—in, sometimes spitting us out, sometimes not, sometimes sucking us back in again.

And again.

INTAKE

When I fall flat on my face it's not spectacular in any way. I just fall on my face. Not quite flat on it, on the whole face. More like fall-on-cheek. I am drunk when it happens but I'm not too drunk. Not fall-on-your-whole-face drunk.

One minute I'm walking on the street, the next, my cheek is hugging the curb. I'm not even walking fast. Or in a zigzag. I just space out and then I'm on the curb. I could do this sober, no problem. Anybody could do this with all the ice around.

I turn around and go to the nearest dive for a pint. I pile up all the change I fished out of my pockets on the table behind the row of beer taps. The bartender shakes his head. I'm sure he has seen my kind many times. Pretty girl, beat-up, broke, with a soiled jacket, hands raw from never wearing gloves. He doesn't say it out loud but I can sense it. Or my prickly drunkenness can sense it.

Nothing further from the truth, I want to tell him. I'm a mother of a lovely baby boy, a writer, a somebody. I live in a real house, not a rental. But then I remember my face. Whatever is going on with it, on it. I don't want to know yet. I can hardly feel it now, still frozen from January's deadly snap.

I shut up. I drink. I thaw. My jaw throbs.

I don't have enough for another beer after that but I end up with one anyhow. Looks like someone took pity. Maybe the bartender. When I try to recall later, the bartender is reduced to head-shaking gestures and the faint green of neon lights from outside.

———

Those are last things that are clear. Either way, all those thoughts comfort me right now.

I lie in bed and it's morning.

I'm feeling my usual sheer fright. The usual sheer fright is due to not recalling much more about the evening beyond the fall, the backpack surviving the fall, and a little bit of the bar afterwards.

I touch the inside of my mouth with my tongue. I instinctively know to reach far back into the back of my mouth, to the left. I feel where there's a dull pain. The pain lives in the last molar. I can move the tooth back and forth with my tongue, make the pain bigger, itchy. The itchiness of it makes me want to keep doing it. I move it with my tongue.

Stop it.

I move it again, imagining I can sense the delicate fibers breaking, detaching themselves from the bone the more I move the tooth.

Stop it.

I want to touch my face. My hand reaches the cheek after sneaking shyly, reluctantly, underneath the sheets.

I hear my boyfriend's light snoring behind me.

So. I'm in bed. Not on the couch or on the floor in the baby's room. And the boyfriend is in bed with me. That means that we probably didn't have a big fight last night and that despite whatever's happened to my face, I'm still human enough to sleep beside.

I slide out of bed as quietly as I possibly can. My clothes are all over the floor, tights in the hallway.

In the bathroom I look in the mirror. No black eye. Not too bad at all. Swollen on the left side and there's a big chunk of skin scraped off along the cheekbone, but nothing serious. I can drape my long hair over it and you won't see a thing.

I get under the shower. My body feels tender all over, but especially on its left side, and I have a hard time bending down when I shave my legs, but I make myself.

Don't be a baby. My hip hurts the most, and when I look down I notice that the skin there is already changing colors. I touch it and it yelps back in pain. Add it to the broken-tooth pain.

It's the bruises that tell the whole tale. They're every drunk's distinctive mark. The map of misfortunes is painted all over our bodies. Blue and black and yellow, like watercolor flowers, or the fresh ones: blossoming red, shy pink.

———

That day, the official intake guy from New Hope calls and asks intrusive questions. When is the last time I had a drink? Do I smoke? How long have I been drinking for? Do I have any offensive tattoos, visible to people?

One that is visible and not offensive: my son's name on my wrist.

What about piercings, anything unusual?

No. Nothing unusual, I say and look up and down my body to double-check.

Do you have frequent and unusual accidents?

No. Yes, I say, feel the soreness inside my mouth as I tell the truth.

You can lie—most people do—but it's better to save your lying energy for other, bigger stuff.

These are just questions, and if you're an addict, chances are you know how to answer them. This is the fate of an addict: people ask over and over because you fail over and over. They want to know everything about you to figure you out and why you are the way you are. They demand every intimate number in your life—falls, injuries, days, drinks, years, partners, hospitalizations—and urges—to harm, to fuck, to die and kill—and everything else that is sacred or secret.

There's no privacy if you're an addict. If you're an addict, people have a right to look through your purses, into your mouth and your eyes. They can draw your blood and check your shit, and for that matter, check inside you, inspect every hole to see if you're lying to them. The only place they don't have access to is your mind, which is why they ask and ask. Your mind is also the part that everyone—including you—is telling you to stay away from. Because it is your mind that is killing you.

———

The intake guy says that any medication I need to bring with me must be blister-packed. To make sure nobody—that means me—tampers with it. You wouldn't believe the things people smuggle in, he laughs.

Like what?

We've found all kinds of drugs, he says. Usually they put them in those ceiling boards so we check their bags right away now but people can get quite creative.

Why would you bring drugs to rehab? I want to ask but I know he'll only think I'm trying to suck up to him. But I really do wonder that. What would be the point?

The intake guy reminds me that I have to be clean and sober for ten days before checking in.

That means from Saturday on, right? I confirm.

He laughs, again, and says that we're so predictable.

Who's *we*? I ask.

We. The addicts. Don't get your knickers in a twist. I'm one of us, been sober for twenty-two years this July.

AA? I guess.

I'm not telling. Do you have any questions?

Yeah, that was my question.

He laughs. Oh, and bring a travel mug. Everybody brings a travel mug. People get worried about germs. It's unnecessary. But bring one anyway.

——

As January slides into February there isn't much left to do before I leave but pack and shop for things like a toothbrush and a prescription refill. I have to tell the pharmacist that I'm going to rehab because he refuses to blister-pack my medication until I give him a reason. Now I can never come back to this pharmacy.

We've arranged for home daycare that I went to check out two weeks before my departure. The daycare is in a private house.

Besides Frankie there's only one other kid, the child of the caretakers. The caretakers are a couple: an obese woman who seems like she's on the edge of a mental breakdown and her obese husband.

The husband is probably a pedophile, we snicker at each other.

Fake laughter.

This stupid remark, an attempt at a joke, is said out of anxiety and makes us even more uncomfortable.

Nothing will happen, my boyfriend says.

Of course not.

ON MY WAY

This is the last time, I tell myself and I actually feel it, I feel that it just might be the last time. I might have a choice, after all. My walk to the store becomes light; it's lighter than it's been in months.

Such relief.

I pick out a bottle of wine and a mickey, joke with the cashier, tell her about the party we're having tonight. Because we're having a party. This time we're really having a party. I can't remember why but everyone my boyfriend knows is invited and for once we lift the alcohol ban in the house. My boyfriend asks me repeatedly if I'm okay with that and I repeatedly say that I'm going to rehab in ten days and then we both feel reassured and then he asks me again.

———

I hide my mickey in the baby's room. I don't need to be overly careful with it but just in case I bury it in the drawer filled with the baby's tiny socks.

The party starts slowly but then it gets bigger than we'd expected. Lots of friends show up. Strangers show up in fancy outfits, some straight from gallery openings, poetry readings, a woman with a man everyone knows is married. I walk in on them making out by the baby's room.

At an earlier point in the evening, I smuggle out the empty mickey and throw it far, far off into the landscape of roofs, from the back balcony.

Later, I sit outside with Camille on a front-porch bench. She gives me sips of her wine, giggling a little. She knows that officially I'm not drinking, she knows about me going away.

She tells me some little story about her past, something about an old fling, a mass of knots that is her former love life.

Camille is at least ten years older than me. She's so gorgeous I often feel like kissing her. Right now I wish I was drunker so that I would get the courage to kiss her. I imagine her husband walking in on us. Joining. He would join. I want to kiss them both. I want to kiss everybody. But I'm not drunk enough.

I take Camille's hand in mine instead of kissing her, then let go when she gives me a squeeze. She goes back to her story about the old fling and, suddenly, I feel so shockingly sober that I can't stand this anymore.

I have to go, I say, get up and leave. This is because I realize something: I can't get any drunker. I'm drinking myself sober.

—

But I keep at it, steadily throughout the night.

I don't discriminate. I drink whatever others are drinking. Rum and Coke, beer, wine. Vodka.

I drink from bottoms of glasses and plastic cups. Because, yes, we had to break out the plastic cups.

I keep one cup filled up with juice by my side at all times, too. My boyfriend stops me periodically and takes tiny sips out of the juice cup and nods approvingly each time.

He declares the party a success.

—

Some of my friends who weren't at the party ask about me going away.

I am cavalier about it, say I'm going to at least get some decent sleep. It's a break from the baby. It's practically a vacation.

I'm going to do some research. For my book, I say to other friends. I'm going to write a book about a woman who's a mom who drinks. Then they send her to rehab.

That's cool, that's cool, say the friends who don't know me well enough to figure out if I'm serious or if this is just something I'm really doing.

Rehab? say some of the friends I met in AA. Probably not a bad idea.

I bristle at this. It's just for three weeks. It's not even *rehab*-rehab.

Whatever helps. Have you thought of going back to meetings?

You mean the cult central? Because you know that AA is a cult.

Right. Whatever works for you.

Judgy-judgy.

Like many addicts I've learned to compartmentalize my friendships: drink with some, get sober with others, never talk about drinking or being sober with yet others, never talk to those I think will get too alarmed if they find out I am drinking again.

The compartmentalization is a useful skill for an addict because it allows me to move from group to group without being caught and confronted. Just like in my twenties when I drank a lot—and when I didn't drink in secret—and used to flit from group to group of people. Just like then, now I socialize with people who won't overlap and compare stories.

If I do socialize. I mostly just stay by myself. I'm detoxing. Spend my days white-knuckling: go for endless walks, change endless diapers, cover my son's beautiful chubby body with endless kisses, feed him mush and formula, watch dozens of movies, read dozens of books to try to distract my insistent brain, to stave off the waiting and wanting.

One weekend before rehab, my friend Angie shows up and insists on taking me to an AA meeting. This is going to be my first meeting in more than a year.

I go because she asks nicely and because I am so bored by being good that I actually consider going to a meeting as something fun to do. I know I'm not going there to learn how not to drink. I'm just going to see what those nutjobs in AA are up to now, I tell myself.

We drive to the meeting in her car. Angie chats and laughs. She doesn't ask how long I've been sober. This is why we're friends. Her friendship doesn't depend on the length of my sobriety. She's just my friend.

Some people in AA tend to stay away when they know you're drinking actively; some try to save you too hard. Some don't even know you're drinking because you cut them off because of your own shame. Some would never think to reach out because you always appear just fine. Sober. Well put together. Strong.

I'm good at appearing strong.

Angie isn't fooled. But she doesn't say anything about it. She instinctively knows not to. Maybe she remembers all too well what it was like to be on my side of things.

———

We drive to the meeting.

I am wearing all black. I'm wearing my hair down. I'm a teenage girl being driven by her mom to a boring family function.

We get there. People shake our hands. The meeting starts.

I am asked to do a reading and I get up to the front of the room and read "How It Works"—something that I've read hundreds of time before. I used to feel this and other AA texts right there, in my gut, in my conviction—if conviction had a place in my body and it happened to be in my gut.

This time I'm just reading words and sentences, sticking them together into a coherent whole. Concentrate on curbing my eastern European accent poking out of certain, tricky words: *balked, earnestness, nil*.

Done reading, I look around the room and notice a cute guy in the second row grinning at me. Victor. A guy I met in the rooms in my former sober, AA life. I grin back at him. Before, I would never do that since I've never considered AA rooms to be places to find cute guys, only recovery, but this time, I'm just here to visit.

Victor stares, unabashedly, as I walk back to my seat.

I say to Angie, I'm really glad I came to this meeting.

She squeezes my hand.

I say, Victor.

She giggles quietly.

The speaker chosen to tell his story at the meeting is not here. The chairperson looks around the room and says, Can anyone volunteer to speak?

Silence.

Angie volunteers to tell her story. She goes up to the front of the room.

She tells her story. She tells it beautifully. She talks about feeling raw, walking around skinless, with her nerves exposed. About the comfort of a drug. The drug providing the skin she so desperately needed.

About staying up for three nights in a row, ODing in the after-hours club.

About getting sober.

Everyone claps when her story is done. I try to cry but can't.

———

Before we part, Angie shows me a white box. In it, there's a little stuffed bear. The bear has wings, a halo and a tag attached to it that says its name is Halo, the bear. Angie says this is her guardian angel bear.

There's a card from Angie in the box too. A card that says I'm supposed to return the bear to Angie once I'm done with rehab. Angie knows about how I pretend to be strong and she's respectful of that, so in her card she says she knows it's cheesy and everything, but the guardian angel bear has helped her when she was trying to get sober in the past.

I want to make a joke about the bear. Something, something, something drunk bear.

But I know that this means a lot to Angie. I say I'm going to return the box and the bear will stay completely sober.

She shakes very slightly when she gives me the box and explains about the bear.

It's going to be okay, I assure her.

She looks at me, big brown eyes scanning my face. Gentle, compassionate eyes. She says in an almost-whisper: I know.

I hope my face shows that I'm not too worried. That I'm relaxed. That this is really sweet. That she has nothing to worry about indeed and neither do I.

That I'm not really scared.

I pull her close and we hug.

———

The long, long days leading up to my departure are a blur. I smoke two packs of cigarettes a day, it seems, and as usual, shop for stupid stuff that I don't need to distract myself. I empty my entire checking account as a result.

I buy four shirts in the same style, four different colors, same boring shirt.

Rock 'n' roll boots with a hundred zippers on them, so many books I'll need three lifetimes to get through them.

I go for manicures and chew off my nail polish almost immediately afterwards. I want to get tattoos, big full-back pieces with skulls and birds in them, anything, any random thing to not think about drinking.

I stay sober for those ten days because I know that this is my last chance and I can't afford to screw up anymore.

The daylight turns from dim to muddy, the trees are shivering, painfully wet, bare; there's dirt and soaked trash everywhere poking out of dirt. March is finally here.

CHECKING IN

On the morning of my departure, I take photographs of my boyfriend holding the baby, both of them trying to look happy. My boyfriend has been wearing glasses since Christmas. The glasses make him seem older, more fragile. As I take pictures, he shouts with pretend cheerfulness to the baby to give Mommy a big smile, give Mommy a big smile, and the baby obeys. The smile is a little unsure but it is lovely: little teeth like tiny pearls glistening with spit as he stretches his cherubic pout. My boyfriend's smile, in contrast, is big and fake and strange-looking against the seriousness of his bespectacled eyes.

My boyfriend cries a few times that morning and I think it's for me and I am touched. He says it's that he's terrified of being able to handle the next few weeks on his own with the baby. This is why he's crying.

———

The baby stays with my sister while my boyfriend takes me to New Hope. We drive along a very gray highway; on its side, rows of warehouses, parking lots and later on fields of broken, frozen wheat and soil and old snow.

———

The rehab building is by a big lake near a hospital. The building is an ugly two-story structure of pale orange brick, greenish paneling, dirty-looking windows, with a chain-fenced yard with two picnic tables and a basketball court outside. There's another building separating it from the lake, possibly a seniors' residence judging by the few wheelchairs with whitehairs sitting outside. There's a parking lot behind the courtyard but there's no access to the lake. A factory on the lake is visible in the distance.

It's starting to rain as we pull into the parking lot, and the boyfriend and I smile to each other, sadly. We are probably thinking the same thing in our helplessly poetic brains: how appropriate, this rain.

He carries my small suitcase into the building while I go to the front desk and sign in. I immediately get cuffed in a plastic hospital bracelet with my name on it. I no longer belong to the world, just this place.

We hug, quickly, and I take a deep, deep breath to inhale his smell as we do. My boyfriend says he loves me. I see his hand going up to his eyes and I tell him to go, leave, get back to Frankie.

Wide leather shoulders. My last glimpse.

After filling out forms and disclosing yet more personal details (names of emergency contacts, names of the child, the spouse, middle names belonging to me, nicknames people should call me, last time I used, what I used, am I on Nicorette, would I like to be) to strangers, I'm finally taken to my room.

The room is big and cold. There's a linoleum floor, two narrow beds with plastic mattress covers and thin, chewed-up hospital blankets. A pillow clearly made out of plastic, rustling in its starched-white case. A rickety night table sits by each bed supporting a lamp with a fluorescent bulb. There's a desk and a metal chair. Two windows with heavy curtains. The overhead lights are fluorescent too. The bathroom is awash in yellow.

My suitcase is placed on one of the beds and I am told to unpack it. There are two women with me. They are watching me unload the suitcase. A couple of shirts, a pair of jeans, nothing fancy; I haven't brought any makeup. I brought some books. The stuffed guardian angel bear from my friend Angie. They flip through the books. What could I have hidden in between the pages of books? Sheets of acid? Powder? They fish out an album with the photos of my son and his father that I printed right before we left this morning. They say my son is cute.

Once the suitcase is empty, one of the women runs her hands against its bottom and opens the zippers on the side. Smart. I recall when I used to keep my mickey in the hidden second bottom of this suitcase last summer.

After they're done, one of them says she's sorry.

No, it's your job, I smile at her.

I'm told to finish unpacking and settle in.

―――――

When the door opens half an hour later, it's as if a force enters, not a girl.

She's tall, in tight jeans, high-heeled boots. She's got a head full of tight curls. She seems to be in the middle of some hilarious story about a fireman. I quickly learn it's someone she's dating, someone who's so dreamy, she says, I just wanna eat him up, oh my god. At this, she bursts out laughing and the two women who come in with her laugh along. They are setting down one giant suitcase each on her bed; the girl has a suitcase too. Three suitcases in total.

She bounces up to me with her hand extended, bracelets clinking madly as we shake, I'm Sade. Like Sad but with an *e*, she says. Like the singer.

Up close she smells of candy and cigarette smoke.

What about this? What's this? one of the women calls.

Oh, that's just my makeup. I have a whole suitcase of makeup, can you believe it? Oh my god, that's my vanilla bodyspray, leave it. Leave it. I just love vanilla, don't you?

The two women take turns sniffing the spray bottle.

There's no alcohol in it, come on you guys, Sad-with-an-*e* laughs.

Sorry, it's the procedure, one of the women explains.

I watch as they unpack loads and loads of clothes: shoes, sweaters, skirts, dresses, underwear in every color imaginable. The third suitcase contains a large comforter and matching sheets. There's a bag of fluffy towels. In the makeup suitcase, there are bags of hair products, which the women say they have to confiscate as it's against the rules. Sade screams once when they shove the hair products in a basket they've brought with them, but stops protesting almost immediately and rolls her eyes at me, saying she should've known better, this is her third time here.

I got kicked out for smoking, right, Mary? she says, Too funny, my god. I got caught, she laughs.

She laughs all the time. Everything is funny.

———

After the women leave, Sade moves her bed so that it's parallel to mine and she starts sticking photographs on the wall beside it. She takes her clothes and all her products to the closet in the hallway where my things hang sadly, sternly.

She talks non-stop.

Why are you here?

Alcohol. I drink too much. I—

I'm a crack ho. But I'm not really a crack ho, oh my god, I hate it. I do a couple of blasts, right, here and there? Right? But I'm not a crack ho. I've only walked the street a few times. This is my son, Jamal, look how cute he is. He's with his babydaddy, John. Oh my god, he's such a bird. He thinks he's better than me. Because he doesn't smoke crack but guess who introduced me to it? Yeah. But now he's all like, he's only doing lines and he thinks he's all that. High-end or something. He's got Jamal today but I've got full custody. So I was supposed to have him but I have to get an apartment with a bedroom for him and I have to be clean for at least a year. And they won't let me see him. Like, you know, John will make plans to drop him off and then he'll cancel last minute and what am I supposed to do? Call the cops? I don't want my boy to hate on him so I say to him, 'Honey, you know that Mommy loves you, right? What do you want to do?' and he'll cry and say, 'I don't know, Mommy, Daddy tells me—' and I'm like, 'What is Daddy telling you?' and he's all scared and he won't answer me. He's with John and his parents and John's got a girlfriend who's pregnant now and I'm like, you'll see what you're getting yourself into, you'll see. Three babies with three different women and he's better than me. He's such a fucking bird. He's going to some stupid cooking school and his parents are paying for it and he's the shit? I was going to get my nursing degree—

———

Three hours into rehab, I'm hiding out in what is known as the Quiet Room. My head is pounding and I'm trying to read but I can't quite see the words on the page, I don't know what any of it means—the words—and I am afraid to go back to my room. At the same time I can't wait to find out more—Sade is better than having a TV in my room. And I don't think about drinking. The rehab is clearly working.

INSIDE

Before supper, the first night, in the women's lounge, we unload our big and little burdens right away: our addictions, boyfriends, babies. I'm surprised at how quickly we reveal ourselves to each other. Then again, none of us are here because we mistook this place for a spa.

My roommate laughs all the time, and the girls huddle around her like a fire. The other crack addict, Donna, is skeletal and shaky and says things in bursts and spurts while playing with the strings of her hoodie. Her teeth are exquisite, white and even. When I compliment her on them, she says she ground her real teeth rotten, these are dentures. She has a thick dressing on her chest that she says—creepily, mysteriously—hides her "special friend."

I bond with other alcoholics. We share stories of hidden bottles. When I mention the liquor-store maps in my head, Tina, one of the alcoholics, laughs so hard she almost falls off the couch. I know exactly what you're talking about, she says.

I say to the women when they ask that I miss my sweet little baby like crazy, but the truth is I feel nothing.

———

The first night, our meal is chicken with vegetables and a cup of watery soup and sticky cake. It's tasteless and two Italian guys are complaining loudly about it. One pushes the plastic tray across the table and yells, It's free and I'll throw a fork in it for you, whoever wants it.

My roommate eats fast, as if she doesn't have any time to waste. It's the only time when she seems to be serious and quiet. She refuses the bread roll and doesn't eat her cake. She points to a nonexistent bulge in her stomach.

Even here, I think, I notice other women doing weird things with food on their plates. Pushing the greasy bits aside, skipping the cake. I do weird things too. I skip the cake. The one person I catch eating everything is a counselor with a round, pretty face. She actually reaches for the abandoned chicken dinner when she thinks no one is looking.

The meal is over in minutes. I escape to the kitchen. I'm alone for a few moments so I orient myself as quickly as I can and finally figure out where the fresh fruit is—I've seen a few people hoarding it already—and I grab a banana. I peel it, break it and eat it fast, fast, possibly inspired by my roommate. I also don't want to eat a banana in front of anyone.

Some of the guys in here are exactly what I'd like to avoid. They're not at all like my boyfriend. The ones capable of banana jokes have arms and legs covered in bad tattoos, rows of even scars. They talk about doing time. They don't talk to one of their ilk because he was a pee-see. I find out later that this is PC, protective custody, which means that he ratted people out or worse.

The other guys I'd like to avoid are the ones in khaki dad pants and sweatshirts that say *My Daughter Goes to Western and All I Got Is This Sweatshirt*. The dad pants smile at you like they're your high school teachers but the joke is on them, because, soon, everyone here will revert to their teenage self and there will be only us versus them, the counselors, when we start getting kicked out for smoking cigarettes.

———

According to our schedules, the days are divided into blocks, with way too much time devoted to meals and meds. According to the schedule, the dinner we've just had should have taken an hour and a half. I spend the rest of the hour and a half listening to more roommate stories in our room. We lie on the beds like girls at summer camp, our sock-clad feet in the air, moving up and down.

She got to New Hope by cab. She says, A friend—not like a boyfriend or anything—drove me here. For free. He's been sober for years. He's a cabbie. He's in AA.

She talks about being on welfare, people lend her money, well, men do, it's no big deal. She says she picks her face, says that's what she is, a picker. She only does it real bad when she's high. She smokes crack and then she picks her face, she imagines there's something underneath her skin, zits waiting to pop up.

And now you'll know what a crackhead looks like, just look at their faces, their jaws, a lot of them are pickers, she says.

I think about my neighborhood back home and all those shady, shuffling people I've always wondered about. We live in a developing area, still full of sadness, the underground above ground, and its people in sweatpants, eyes flicking away. Now I will look at their faces and I will know.

———

At night, I toss and turn on the terrible bed with the plastic sheets and pillow. I fall asleep, finally, but am woken up by the most horrible stench coming from my roommate's corner of the room. I hide under the towel that serves as an extra blanket and inhale my own familiar sweat and sour heat mixed with deodorant. Better.

A couple of hours later, I wake up again. The stench is gone. So is my roommate. She comes back and gets into bed. I hear wrappers being opened and crunching—eating—and one small burp.

———

The next day, in the first women's group meeting, called "Grief and Loss," I find out that I am dissociated.

Dissociated.

It rings true but so what? So what that now I know what it is that I am?

The group facilitator says to give myself some time, see what else comes out.

After the meeting is over, I think about following her. I want to tell her that the other thing that might come out is a flood of love and happiness, what I felt when my son was born, and that it'll sweep me away; it's so much bigger than me. And I can't take it. And, at home, I have to drink to calm it down.

I don't say anything like that to her, partly because I can just imagine her getting all hot and wet over my poetic language. Everything in here sounds like poetry, or rather, sentiment. Everyone—counselors and some clients—uses words and phrases like *stay in the present, enjoy the journey, non-judgmental, believe, miracles, hope, serenity.*

"Believe in miracles, hope and serenity."

The group meetings themselves carry combination names. Besides "Grief and Loss," there's "Wellness and Spirit," "Feelings and Triggers," "Refusal Role Play (Clients practice refusing offers of substance in high-risk situations)," "Anti-Boredom (Activities for combating boredom while in treatment and recovery)." Crap like that.

I know some of these words and phrases from before—both from AA meetings and my harm reduction group. They puzzle and irritate me just the same. I'm not the only one.

At lunch the next day, one of the guys comes up to me and says, How was your "Grief and Loss?" and we both giggle.

I know that I should be grieving Frankie's first few months, how I will never get them back, I tell the guy.

He says he talked about his babymama in his "Grief and Loss." How she was such a bitch to him and she used to be totally different before she became a junkie.

———

Nobody goes outside.

There's not much of an outside to speak of.

In the women's section, there's a garden that the men don't have access to, and we're told to go and check it out. The garden area is the size of Frankie's crib. There are cameras above the door. There's a wooden fence, the magic fence that I'm not supposed to jump or I'll get kicked out. I can see what's behind it. Houses and cars on a quiet residential street. I have no desire to jump the fence, not even to see what might happen.

Nobody checks out the garden except for me. The other women spend most of their free time on payphones talking to boyfriends or in the lounge watching TV.

———

Inside, I wear my rehab costume. I've got runners and sweatpants and headbands. Stuff celebrity addicts wear on reality TV. The rest of the girls—because that's what I call them, and that's what we are in here, *girls*, in this strange boarding school—dress just like they would outside. Everyone has a pedicure, even the shaky, skinny crackhead, Donna. There's a new girl, Alex, who is introduced to us after lunch on the second day. She is skinny and doesn't talk. She keeps her hands hidden in her sleeves, is probably the only other sloppy dresser besides me. She's freezing all the time. She's coming off Oxys, Sade says.

———

Over the first few nights, my roommate's gassy condition dissipates and it's possible to breathe again at night. She tells me this is a common side effect of a long-term user, this horrible gas.

I learn so much from her all the time. One evening she tells me about being up for ten days straight and losing control of her left arm—it kept jerking and flinging itself forward, against her will. She thinks it must've been a mini-stroke.

Naturally she laughs about it and I laugh with her as she re-enacts those bizarre, jerky movements with her other arm. The left one never fully recovered and will still spasm uncontrollably, and her hand clenches painfully when she's agitated. She says it's better not to mess with it. She says her sugar daddy makes fun of it.

Your sugar daddy?

Well, how else do you think I keep my head above water?

———

Before meals and group activities, my roommate runs around nude trying on different combinations of tight sweaters and leggings. She changes her outfits three, four times a day. It occurs to me that this is a clever tactic, just one of the ways to divide our days further, keep busy. Sade's telling me more about herself in furious bits and pieces. The stories are complete with re-enactments of how people were standing or leaning, voices and how they yelled at each other, even how some bitches got slapped.

She talks about her addiction too, how she spent a month in a crackhouse once and one morning came to with her face and hands covered in bedbug bites. That experience ruined crack smoking for her. Now she sees the bugs whenever she does blasts.

———

I have to express milk, so standing in our little bathroom, I pump my breasts, letting the milk drip into the travel mug. The travel mug has come in handy after all. I told my roommate about what I have to do and she's curious about how it's done without a pump. I invite her to watch as I squeeze around my nipple, hard, until a few tiny white threads of milk erupt on the surface, combined with some watery-white droplets.

Wow, is all she says, and I point my nipple downward to direct the stream into the travel mug and I keep squeezing. Because it comes out in such small amounts, I need to do this for a long time—press, squeeze, press—to get as much as one-third of the mug filled.

My roommate says she never breastfed her kids. She was too out of it. She never breastfed her first either. The baby died two weeks after being born. She says this breezily, in a matter-of-fact way. It's just a fact from her past, as is the fact that her mother is dead and so is her real father.

Everyone is dead, pretty much, she says, sounding a little surprised. Then she bursts out laughing. I'm sorry, I'm sorry, I don't know what's wrong with me. It was a long time ago, when my baby died, she says when she calms down.

She says, I was fourteen when I got pregnant. I thought you only took the birth-control pill once and you were good to go.

She laughs again, and I join her because this *is* kind of funny.

———

After breakfast, men and women meet in the Group Room upstairs and go over goals for the day with the counselors. We go around the room and speak about our goal when it's our turn. The goals are simple: to call parents, to call boyfriends, to exercise, to finally start reading a book.

I'm going to call Frankie, I say, even though I brought no phone cards. But this is supposed to be a goal, right? So I should do anything I can to achieve it, even steal, right? I don't know where this thinking comes from. Perhaps it's all the thieves and other petty criminals in here who talk about stealing and holding up convenience stores. On the other hand, I don't know if I should believe anybody in here anyway. The angel-faced Alex who in one of our earlier trust exercises confesses to being an escort at an agency? Please. She has zero social skills. She barely talks and spends most of the time chewing on the ends of her sweatshirt sleeves. I have a hard time picturing her as a great seductress.

After the goals, we usually have a fifteen-minute anti-smoking session with an overeager woman whose father died of lung cancer. She is one of the nurses here.

She brings DVDs and clippings about tobacco-related deaths. She's full of curious statistics, like comparisons of deaths related to tobacco consumption versus deaths due to homicide or car accidents.

She plays movies in which people with holes in their throats and oxygen tanks on wheels talk about wishing they had had better foresight.

The only person relatively interested in these workshops is the main dad pants guy, who's the first person ever to come to New Hope for help with a smoking habit.

He asks questions. He's the one who's usually silent during our other workshops, where people talk about visiting the afterlife a couple of times thanks to overconsumption of heroin.

In the tobacco workshops, Dad Pants gets to talk.

———

After the morning sessions, we're given the choice of staying in the Group Room with everyone or going to a one-on-one meeting with a counselor. Most people choose to stay. I stay almost every time.

In the Group Room we're taught breathing exercises and meditation techniques. The first week they even bring in an acupuncture guy who explains that he will put needles in our ears to stimulate positive energies that will help us to relax, deal with our cravings and help us sleep. I let him stick ten tiny needles in my ear. Within seconds, they detach themselves, one by one, from my skin with a minuscule silver prickle.

It means that my energy lines are sufficiently stimulated, the acupuncture guy tells me in an excited whisper.

Plinky-plonky Asian music plays gently around us. Most people have their eyes closed.

Alex, the anorexic escort in her giant white hoodie and white jogging pants that cover her feet, sits with her back to me, facing the window. Her hair is long and wispy, lit up from the window like a halo. Next to her sits an old heroin addict, a lovable goofy guy in his forties or fifties or sixties. He's been following the anorexic around and I can't decide if he wants to have sex with her or protect her. Probably both.

———

I close my eyes but I can't relax. I want to jump up and run out of the room. I want to scream and break through this stupid waterfall music and the quiet giggling and whispering echoing from all corners.

———

I open my eyes.

I see Alex and the old guy in front of me. Now he's touching her shoulder gently, carefully. He calls for the acupuncture guy in a whisper and explains that a needle fell out of her ear. He's looking down on the floor.

The acupuncture guy walks up to Alex and bends down too.

Now they're both like this, bowing down on each side of her. It's the coronation of the Virgin, the two guys moving hands gently, without touching, around her head and delicate shoulders. She sits still in the light.

Watching this, I feel myself calming down a bit, for the first time.

POST-TRAUMATIC STRESS DISORDERS

n the afternoons men and women attend separate group meetings where they discuss issues more specific to their genders. The women meet in the lounge downstairs; downstairs is also where all the women have their bedrooms. The men have no access to this floor.

During one of the early sessions I learn that I'm the only one with an infant, and the women ask to see my son's pictures, again. He's so beautiful, they all say. The counselor who's with us says, You're so lucky you're doing this now. Your sobriety, it's the best gift you can give him.

I disagree. I tell her the best gift I could have given him would have been not picking up that first drink at the party we had to welcome him to the world. Or maybe the drink I had in Warsaw before I even knew I was pregnant? Or the very first drink I ever had?

But there's no sense beating yourself up about it now, is there? she says and hands me back the album after everyone has looked at it.

I haven't really looked at these pictures since coming here, I'm just showing them to people. There's no lying on the bed, staring at my baby's face, crying.

It's not that I don't care. I'm still numb, locked inside myself.

———

After this group session is over, the counselor asks me to meet with her one-on-one. She asks how I feel when I look at his pictures, possibly picking up on my keeping the album shut close on my lap once it made it back to me.

I don't know, I say.

The counselor says that maybe I'm dissociating. It's a normal part of recovery. It happens even in the first week of recovery.

Dissociating? Like how?

You're not entirely in touch with the painful emotions, you're protecting yourself from the pain that the pictures may bring. And the dissociation may be due to post-traumatic stress disorder.

Like what? I say.

Birth. Even birth. Even birth can cause post-traumatic stress disorder.

This is one of those things that therapists talk about. Post-traumatic stress disorder. Anything can cause post-traumatic stress disorder, it seems. It's not just for Iraqi war veterans anymore. Becoming a new mother, immigrating, getting married, getting fired—everything causes post-traumatic stress disorder if the mind isn't ready to absorb it. We're a walking fucking trauma, all of us.

Isn't the human condition a post-traumatic stress disorder? I ask the counselor.

She says, In a way it is. That's a good way of seeing it.

Really.

———

Post-traumatic stress disorder or not, I'm able to appreciate the photographs of my son for their aesthetic value. He's a beautiful child. In my mind he is exactly the way he is in those pictures—two-dimensional, perfect, silent. Not real. Before falling asleep that night, I try to imagine some other details to make the picture a little fuller: how his chubby feet smash against the floor when he's excited.

———

There are two phones downstairs where the women are. Both phones are occupied constantly between meals and activities. Donna the white-toothed crack addict is on the phone the most, especially in the evening when her lover is back from work. She enters the women's lounge with a glum face every evening after she finishes her calls. From the beginning, she's been missing meals and even some group meetings to answer the phone, which seems to be ringing for her all the time. Her man is calling and threatening to take up with someone else if she doesn't return to him soon. He's doing coke all the time, she cries. I'm not sure if the crying is for him or for all the coke being done without her around.

He doesn't know how to take care of himself, ya know? she explains further, and nobody thinks this is weird.

I do. I think it's awful and weird because if she goes back to her man to serve him, she'll be dead soon. She takes the dressing off her chest on that teary evening too and reveals to us her "special friend," an IV catheter in her chest.

I had cancer. It's for chemo, she explains.

What do you mean? asks Tina, the alcoholic. They put the chemo drugs in there?

Aha, she says.

Did you ever put—?

Oh yeah, Donna says, I didn't want them to remove it, ya know?

The phone calls from her man increase throughout the day, right before the weekend. He's now calling the front desk, we find out from my roommate, who knows everything. He calls the counselors and he calls both phones available to us on the women's floor. This creates lots of tension because suddenly nobody else can get through and we use the phone calls to break the monotony of the day. Donna apologizes all the time. But we all grow sick of her and her apologies and her crazy boyfriend.

She leaves that evening, on Friday. Sade says something about this Friday being the social assistance day.

What do you mean?

Her welfare check? The check came, he wants her to cash it, buy rock, goodbye, so long, she giggles. Sade says Donna's man came to pick her up.

The women meet in the lounge to talk about what happened with Donna. Donna has written on the blackboard in the lounge that she'll never forget us and that she has learned a lot in these past few days, more than she has in years.

I don't believe for one second that she'll stay clean. She learned nothing. We addicts often learn nothing. Which is why we keep going back. Or dying.

LEARNING

t's the morning after Donna leaves and I find her absence at breakfast jarring but also hopeful. We can leave here. Of course we can leave here. One of the counselors says that Donna's leaving like this is a normal part of recovery. Overconfidence is a normal part of recovery.

After breakfast, from the cafeteria, I watch the lake and its shimmering gray-blue waters. It's a sunny day and there are people walking on the boardwalk. Couples and families. I'm sure there's at least one alcoholic or drug addict among them. There must be at least one mother pushing a stroller, a mother who's also sipping discreetly out of her coffee mug, eyes darting side to side. Perhaps not. Perhaps I was one of a kind and it's all sweet and proper on the other side of the fence. I sit by the window and watch the tiny people move about as I peel orange after orange—they have the most amazing, delicious oranges here at the New Hope center.

———

Alex the teenage escort has meltdowns all the time. In women's groups she's mostly quiet but then will burst into tears or swear at the counselors—but not really *at them*, it seems; it's more of a general fuck-off with her emotions playing out briefly on her tiny anorexic face, big mouth quivering before she suddenly shuts down. Once she shuts down, she's calm, almost comatose with blank eyes. If asked a question she shrugs—that universal teenage movement intended to crush everyone around her. I'm dying to hear her escort stories—I feel bad about it but I'm dying to hear them nonetheless—but it seems she's unable to formulate sentences that go beyond, "This is so fucked" or "I fucking hate this shit." Even after coming off the Oxys she seems to be in a fragile state, hands still hidden in sleeves, eyes outlined in so much black she looks like a sick panda. My roommate tries to get her to talk but even she gets discouraged after too many grunting answers.

I wonder if she has brain damage, but I know she doesn't because I've heard bits and pieces of conversations she has at the dining room table during meals, stuff about music she likes, and she's surprisingly eloquent.

She only talks to guys, I mention to Sade.

Yeah, she's young, dumb and full of cum, my roommate says.

Since she's the youngest girl in here, perhaps she's just acting the part. She and I share a counselor, but I never get to see my counselor because Alex is in her office crying all the time. One time I watch her throw her MP3 player on the floor in the counselor's office, then pick it up and throw it with more force so that it smashes. The counselor sits in her chair and watches this. She looks up. Our eyes lock, and she gives me a sad smile.

Well, at last it's entertaining, I think to myself, though I'm still pissed off that the little bitch is stealing my time with the counselor. That's how bored I'm starting to get—I begin to look forward to my one-on-one sessions with a counselor.

I entertain the thought of grabbing a couple of oranges from the kitchen and going downstairs to the basketball court and then throwing them at the counselor's window. Alex could go on smashing things inside her office and I'd do it outside. Maybe we could drive the counselor to drinking or using Oxys.

———

Because I can't get to see my counselor again, that night I go to the group meeting, where we're told about a test we'll be doing to see how best we can get along with each other. This is interesting because by now we all know each other and it's not like we need any more icebreakers. I bring this up and am told that I can always use True Colors results in the real world.

We're given sheets of paper and are told to answer yes or no to statements such as: I prefer my desk to be organized, I enjoy meeting new people. I write in my own statement, perhaps inspired by Alex's bratty behavior: I shit only when absolutely necessary.

After the questionnaire, we look at pictures that are supposed to represent us and our values, badly done drawings of mimes (you like art!), chessboards (you are analytical!) and such. After all of this is done, the counselors promise, we'll be assigned a color, which will correspond to our personality and suggest possible alliances and potential landmines in each other. I find out I'm

Green-Blue. Sade is Gold and she's very proud of herself, is shouting to everyone that Golds are the best.

———

We are given worksheets where we have to draw a line, from the time we were born to age one hundred. I look at the line and see that in my case I can look forward to sixty-eight years of possibly clean, happy life if I stay with the program and die at one hundred.

And it makes me think of now—the hours of boredom, the hours of obsessing over dumb teen bitches, the hours of personality tests. The now, it's so tiny, I can't actually subtract it from all the time in the rest of my life that I will get to spend with Frankie. It's nothing, barely a speck on the lifeline.

See? my counselor says, when I finally do get to see her the next day. If I hadn't gone to rehab I could have even more days to subtract, perhaps even years. In retrospect—she promises—this will seem like a small sacrifice for a much greater reward.

I know, I know, I tell her, but I still can't justify finding out that I'm Green-Blue—analytical, composed, artistic, loyal—on a personality scale while my breasts swell up with milk.

Where's Frankie now? she says, and it feels like blasphemy to hear her say his name, as if she actually knows him. I try to guess if she's being mean, or if she truly doesn't know. She smiles encouragingly. She wears the peace symbol around her neck.

With his dad.

And how is Frankie?

Fine, I'm sure.

Of course, of course. She pats my hand quickly and lets go.

Do you have any kids? I ask her, and she says she does: a boy and a girl.

This counselor's office, like every other counselor's office, is decorated with inspirational sayings and words carved out in wood plaques.

She asks me what I would like to work on from this peculiar one-on-one menu: Relapse Prevention, Daily Living or Managing Stress?

I don't know, I say.

I've noticed you've been looking at the words on my wall. Is there one you'd like to talk about?

I want to talk about one word that I see on her wall. I say, Believe.

What do you believe in?

I believe that I can have a regular life. I believe I can be a good mom, I can repair my relationship, get back to doing things I enjoy.

She looks so pleased. That's so great, she says. And how about another word? How about Hope? What do you hope for?

That I'll stick to it, that's all. But I'm scared that I will get tempted again. I think about alcohol a lot. I miss it.

And that's an okay feeling, the counselor says. Thank you for your honesty.

I miss it a lot, you don't understand. I think I'll be able to have a glass of wine or two, fine.

You're still in love with it, she says.

In love?

It can be like a former husband or an ex-boyfriend, don't you think? That guy that you never got over?

I try to think of guys I never got over. I was drunk every time. They all blend into some kind of Godzilla-guy monstrosity I never got over.

I suppose, I say. There's always a tiny sliver of hope that we'll get back together, alcohol and me, even if for just one more naked weekend, just one more night. This can't be over, can it?

Well, that's up to you, certainly. You don't have to answer all his calls.

Whose calls?

Your lover's. The one who got away.

Right. I don't. But what if he keeps calling? I change the number and he keeps calling. I hang up on him, and he calls me right back. That's the kind of guy he is. But even if he were to finally give up, I myself have a hard time with finality, I don't want things to just end. Or, worse, to pretend that they've ended. I don't understand how that happens—something *is* but I have to pretend it *isn't*. Like the alcohol is always there. It *is*. It's not *isn't*.

The counselor nods.

Like the teenage Alex, I've given in to strange anger here in this office, with this grown-up nodding smilingly at me. I think: She's not the most attractive woman. She's got eyelashless eyes, the face of a stunned bird.

I immediately feel guilty for thinking that and think of saying something that will please her. So I say, I guess I can just *pretend* that it's not there. One-day-at-a-time thing, right?

That's the idea, she says, if you can get your head around it, or even if you can't, you can just choose not to try to get your head around it for one day. Just tell yourself you're going to think about it tomorrow and until then stay sober. And then you can go through the same routine the next day. And the next.

I'm lost again. How do I not think about it in the first place? Like, is there a way to just erase that first thought?

You might have to start first thing in the morning, she tells me. That's why a lot of people pray first thing in the morning. You've no defences when you first wake up, so you quickly say your little mantra, a prayer, whatever you say, and then you're set for the day. It's like you've built a wall for the day. And it's harder for those sorts of thoughts to penetrate that wall.

Aha. In my mind Godzilla is smashing a wall, a giant red telephone is answered by a bird in a dress. Then Godzilla is on his knees, praying. Then the bird flies away.

THE COMMUNITY

The counselors refer to us addicts as a "community," as in: "This community doesn't have anyone with special needs, unlike the community three communities ago." After a week, our community has more or less gelled. A couple of cliques form, based on different commonalities such as heritage, substance of choice, age or musical preference. The closest bond seems to form between the opiate users. The drunks and crackheads are all over the place.

The Italians stick together too, even though they do divide themselves within their own group. There are three Neapolitans and one Sicilian. The Neapolitans call the Sicilian "dirty" behind his back.

I don't feel particularly close to anyone so sometimes I just tag along with my roommate, who has a lot of followers and enemies by the end of the first week.

She moves constantly and is everywhere. She complains about being bored and in the beginning of week two pulls one of the Neapolitans, Donicio, into a bathroom where she shows him her breasts. She comes back to the room to report on his reaction—he was happy, upset, then begging—and says it makes her feel—she can't think of the word.

Powerful, I suggest.

She loves the word. Forgets it the next minute. Remembers: Superior.

During the second week, my roommate and Tina, the alcoholic who has liquor-store maps in her head just like I do, start working out. There's a small, crappy gym with two treadmills, a rowing machine and a couple of yoga mats. It's right beside the cafeteria and nobody pays attention to it until those two start going. They get up early, before breakfast, and every morning I get woken up by Sade singing at the top of her lungs in the shower when she gets back an hour later.

It's so much fun, she tells me as she runs around naked trying on different bra and panty combinations. I feel great. I feel so good, she bursts out laughing, so-o-o good.

So I start going with them.

It turns out my roommate mostly just lies on the yoga mat with her ass in the air, telling stories that make her laugh. If Donicio happens to be walking by—and I realize quickly that he happens to be walking by every morning—she asks him to help her stretch. This means that he gets to lean against her ass or leg as they grunt and giggle, making Tina shout at them to go get a room.

———

Despite being hopelessly out of shape, I get right into working out. Most of the time, I sit on the rowing machine with the poster of the human muscular system in front of me on the wall, right beside a poster with a guy in a canoe with a slogan about pushing to your limits. We push to our limits together.

After a couple of days, once I get used to the rhythm and the workings of the machine, I start to enjoy what I'm doing even more. I concentrate on feeling my muscles inside my body. I visualize them tensing up and expanding and moving as if I were a machine myself. It takes some amount of coordination and concentration to be able to execute all the moves properly, and I like that I don't have to focus on anything else around me, especially all the action on the floor with Sade and Donicio.

Rowing, I think of my future. I imagine myself becoming the sort of person who is disciplined enough to get up in the morning to go to the gym. The sort of person who, if she gets high at all, it's from all the endorphins that kick in after working out.

I'm the last person to leave the gym in the mornings. Sometimes the older Neapolitan, Marco, joins me near the end of my sessions. He doesn't talk. Just runs silently and steadily, 6.0, no incline, twenty minutes a pop. Have a nice day, he says every time he leaves, as if he were actually going somewhere else from here instead of staying in this building with all the other addicts.

One morning, near the end of the second week, Donicio is waiting outside the gym.

I'm waiting for you, he says. He grabs me as I try to get by and presses himself against me. I'm so surprised that I don't do anything to stop him. I like it. I enjoy his hard-on against my body, close my eyes when his face gets closer.

He says something that sounds like, I knew it.

I snap out of it. I open my eyes and tell him to get lost. For a moment I'm scared that he's going to do something crazy, like hit me. He just stares at me for a bit and then walks away without saying anything.

I say nothing to Sade. I'm not even sure it happened when I think about it later.

———

The weekends are the worst. As the second weekend approaches I already know how badly they drag on. I borrow phone cards and talk to my boyfriend a few times. We talk briefly and don't say much to each other. I tell him I want to go home. He tells me there's not that much time left. I tell him everyone is crazy here. He says nothing. I tell him I want to go home. He says he loves me. He tells me there's not that much time left . . .

There's one quiet guy whom everyone calls the Priest; he is calm and personable. It's hard to believe that he drinks at home and rents hookers. He's working on his master's thesis in order to become a full-fledged minister. He may be going to jail for many years after getting out of rehab. He caused an accident while driving drunk—he killed a man. He never says any more about it, just that he killed a man while driving.

In the cafeteria, on weekends, the Priest talks to people about God. He must miss being able to go to church, I suppose. The former inmates like him. Many of them have crosses or rosaries tattooed onto their bodies. They show them off to the Priest. I guess they want to impress, but he looks slightly alarmed when another bicep is flexed right underneath his nose in the name of Jesus.

———

Because the group activities are fewer on weekends, there's even more time to think. I spend most of it thinking about Frankie. Nothing specific, just recalling his smell and the way he sighs or babbles, and how his fat, pink body feels against mine.

It's perhaps because of these constant thoughts that I end up milking myself all the time; my travel mug is never used for coffee.

When I get sick of thinking about Frankie I go to the gym again and again. I become obsessed with feeling my body move and I go back to the gym throughout the day, not only to kill time but also because this is the first thing in months that has made me feel somewhat alive.

When I get sick of the gym, I try to read. But mostly I just end up staring at Frankie's pictures until I feel sleepy enough to pass out.

I sleep a lot.

———

The roommate bounces in and out. She continues to feed me tidbits of her colorful bio—the number of men in her life grows exponentially—and also alters previous details. The sugar daddy turns out to be one of many. There are big, terrifying parts of her story too that make her face scrunch up a little, like the time when she tried to cut her ex's throat.

On weekends, we watch a lot of TV. We watch *Celebrity Rehab*.

On *Celebrity Rehab*, the addicts watch TV. It's a little bit like watching yourself on TV watching TV.

The long, stretchy days seem to be the worst for Alex, who doesn't seem to get better. She cries almost all the time. When she's not upstairs talking to guys about music, she sits in the women's lounge, in the same spot, knees under her chin, balled-up Kleenex all around her. We try to talk to her but she doesn't reply, so we leave her alone, just let her sit there and cry in peace.

———

When we're completely sick of each other, we go up to the cafeteria or the rooms upstairs where there are men. The men are not allowed in our section of the building, but we can go where we please.

There are twice as many men as women. Eventually every woman in here gets a follower or two or three. It's not a big surprise—we're a bunch of bored animals. We're horny animals. We're sober animals.

My followers change day to day, with the exception of a guy named Sebastian who makes sure to sit beside me at every meal and bring me cutlery, salt, pepper and napkins. He has a small face, bunched up in the middle of a small head. His hair is a strange shade of blond, almost yellow. Maybe he dyes it. I can't tell his age. He seems young, younger than me. He says that I'm gorgeous and I say thank you and we leave it at that. Sometimes he asks me if I think he's sexy and I say yes and we leave it at that.

Besides some half-assed flirting, I try to keep to myself.

But there are women here who seem to have come to find life partners. Once in a while you walk in on someone just turning their face away from a kiss, or a whisper, or fingertips brushing against fingertips one last time before letting go.

Besides Sade, Donicio is also involved with one of the older alcoholics, the elementary-school teacher, Charlotte, who drives drunk. She follows him around. She's got a beautiful face but a shapeless, sloppy body that she drags along instead of walking it.

The more Donicio ignores her, the more she talks about her dilemma—to leave her fiancé for him or not. As if someone—Donicio presumably—actually gave her this choice.

She talks about this in all of our women's group meetings. She says, "He's always doing this" and "He's like this all the time," or "That's so like him," as if they've spent a lifetime together, not just a week and a bit. She says he's a great kisser. She sits beside him during every meal, getting up to fetch him condiments or drinks whenever he grunts at her.

My roommate calls her the Wife. In the next breath, she says that Donicio's penis tastes a little like pee but she doesn't mind. She says this late, at night, after we go through the things that we've done over the weekend. She asks me if I think she's a total slut.

REHAB HOCUS-POCUS

Besides acupuncture and meditation, we're introduced to other magical practices that are supposed to help set us straight. In the beginning of week three—our last week here—in mixed group, we're told to tap around our eyes and on our knuckles, with our fingers, saying things like: Even though I have a sore foot, I completely and utterly accept myself. Besides tapping, we also have to hum and count out loud to five. We are concentrating our energies so that we can help someone with whatever is ailing him or her.

We tap for one of the alcoholic men with a sore foot, for the Priest's twisted shoulder and for Donicio's burnt tongue.

The tapping facilitator wants to know if there's anyone else we need to gather our tapping forces for. I've had a mild toothache for a few days now but I don't say anything about it. When it comes to teeth, I prefer to stick to dentistry, rather than magic.

The practice is called Emotional Freedom Technique Tapping Therapy, and the facilitator is wild with enthusiasm. She tells us stories—fragments of stories, really, as she's too hyper to finish them—and she jumps from one anecdote to another like a crazed butterfly, trying to convince us that tapping will cure anything from cancer to addiction to a bad mood or a sore toe.

She says things like, This guy, he was a scientist and his wife dragged him to an EFT workshop and there was no way he was going to believe and on their way home—God, I still feel goosebumps when I tell you this story—he touched his neck where the lump was and it was gone. And my friend Helen, she met a man who used it to help her get over her anxiety—

For the next two days, people are talking about tapping away their cravings, then someone makes a joke about tapping away judges and dealers. By the end of day two, most of us forget the order of the tapping sequence and nobody mentions it again.

———

At the beginning of week three, I get a letter from my boyfriend. He writes about Frankie, how he's doing. He doesn't write about himself at all. It's so kind of him to write me here, I think, and what a wonderful partner he is. He's going to make some lucky woman very happy.

I reread the letter a dozen times. He writes that Frankie has outgrown some of his clothes as if it's been months instead of days, and they had to do a big shopping trip, Frankie and him. Frankie's head is almost as big as a grown-up's and he gets cuter and teethier with every day, he writes, again, as if months have passed.

My roommate sits on the edge of my plastic mattress—it finally occurs to me that it's plastic so that it'll be easier to wash off all of the addict sweat—and she waits for me to stop talking, first time she actually lets me say something.

You'll get him back, don't worry, she says, and I don't know who she means.

It worked out with my babydaddy to get my son back. And as soon as I find a job I can talk to CeeEss again to see if I can get custody back. I need six months clean and a real job.

CeeEss?

Child Services.

I realize that she means Frankie, that she thinks he's been taken away from me by my boyfriend. I don't know why but I don't correct her.

On the wall behind her there's a whole slew of photos of Sade with different women—girlfriends and sisters—in bikinis, holding drinks with umbrellas in them. Then there are various photographs of Sade posing with different children.

Which one is Jamal? I ask.

She points to a little boy with a lazy eye holding hands with a skinny teenager dressed up as a Christmas elf, and a picture of the same boy sitting stiffly on a fat Santa knee, looking directly into the camera, not smiling, this time his eyes are perfectly aligned.

He's really special, my little boy. He is not into sports but he can do anything. It's amazing. We bought him a Transformer for Christmas and it was supposed to be for nine-year-olds but he begged us so I said let's get it, and he just put it together in minutes.

Sade's face glows at me and I shake my head as if I can't believe it and she nods oh yes, yes, yes, and I decide I love my roommate a little bit right then even though I'm too lazy to correct her about my life.

_____

Sometimes I force myself to write about things that I'm going through right now. My hand, so used to typing, is frustratingly slow, never really catching up with my thoughts. So I try to just write about what I can filter through and catch, barely—bits and pieces of conversations, scraps of behaviors, the way faces look when being lectured about tobacco instead of being allowed to sleep in.

_____

The lack of things to do and the co-ed setup affects even the cool-headed alcoholic Tina, who starts flirting, aggressively, with Kevin, one of the night counselors.

Like me, she hadn't brought any makeup with her, so she makes a long list for the delivery services to get lipliners and eyeliners from the local pharmacy. I order packs of gum, which I chew all the time, ruining my broken teeth even more.

_____

During our last week, Tina paints her face every evening before Kevin comes down to the women's lounge to remind us of the ten o'clock curfew.

She lies stretched out on the couch, staring at him and asking him to reveal to us whether he used to be an addict. She asks for gossip about other counselors.

Her face is no longer swollen from booze and her eyes are bright and blue in the forest of thick mascara that actually suits her.

She lisps a little when she talks. She never lisps to us but she lisps to him.

She says he's so cute.

Kevin is polite and laughs politely. He says nothing back to the cute comment. He says very little at all. His arms are tattooed just like the former inmates'—raw ink with thick, sometimes shaky lines.

Tina tells Kevin that she loves him and he wishes us a good night and reminds us that we've only a few minutes left before bedtime.

———

We watch him one afternoon twist and hold the arms of one of the heavily tattooed guys behind his back. The guy has been caught giving Tylenol 4s to his roommate, Dad Pants, who's never done drugs before. Both get kicked out. I never knew that Tylenol even went above 3.

ALEX

Alex, the teenage anorexic escort, gets kicked out three days before rehab is over.

We're not supposed to go to each other's rooms but I go into hers when I find out about it.

She's packing. Just throwing her things into a large suitcase and crying. Boxes of diuretic tea and Sweet'N Low, which I'm not sure how she managed to smuggle in. They could be full of drugs, those sachets, packets and packets of powdered shit in them.

They've found cigarettes on her, she says, and now she has to go back to the fucking detox and this one, it's the worst place on ear-r-r-rth, she bawls.

It's just detox, I say.

On the night table beside her bed there's a picture of a man in a coffin.

What the hell?

She says it's her dad. Dead dad. She says he used to smack her but he was her idol and she started shooting up and eating pills when he died.

And this detox is fucking hell, she says, that's all you need to know. The men there are fucking insane.

I imagine her tiny frame getting gang raped there or worse. I'm not sure what's worse.

To distract myself and her, I think about asking her about her dad dying and her shooting up, but then I snap out of it—what am I trying to do anyway, fix her?

I take crumpled clothes out of her suitcase and fold them and put them back into the suitcase as she paces the room alternating between crying and cursing.

———

I find out later that during this time, upstairs in the cafeteria, her biggest fan, the older Neapolitan, Marco, is pulling paintings off the walls and throwing chairs around. Downstairs, my counselor says that outbursts like that are a normal part of recovery.

———

Later, after they're both gone, everyone is saying that they will most likely use together.

———

Alex being kicked out starts a strange three-day chaos, with the sexual frenzy upstairs, in the common room, at an all-time high now, with people suddenly smelling of tobacco and no longer trying to hide it.

I hide in my room most of the time.

My roommate has exposed her boobs to at least three men that I know of, but she always goes back to her Neapolitan junkie, Donicio, and we all watch her make him salads and fetch him coffee during meals just like Charlotte, the elementary-school teacher whom she called the Wife. Charlotte isn't here anymore to see it. Charlotte hasn't made it to the end either, on account of her man back home asking her to marry him over the phone before week three.

———

The closer to the end, the more I retreat inside myself.

But this time it's different.

Maybe it's because it's just me and no Frankie and no booze, it seems as if I finally have the room to notice myself.

In our final session, my counselor says it's a good feeling, the one I have, of noticing myself, but she pretty much says this about anything—good or bad. She has time to see me all the time, now that Alex is gone.

The person I notice, me, is a person in progress, the counselor explains before I leave her office.

I'm not sure what she means by that. I admit to myself that I'm unfinished in some areas, just like everybody else. And in other areas I seem to be dead, like the part of me that died when I moved here from another country.

I no longer feel that I've come from anywhere. I'm just here. I'm still hanging on to illusions, such as my relationship with my boyfriend. The important thing is that I'm not completely irreversible. Sober, I feel that I can be fixed in some places, such as with my relationship. I even get a sliver of hope, right near the end of my stay, and this is more hope than I've had for months. The feeling of being underwater is still present—the almost palatable sensation that I'm not completely tuned in, that I'm missing something, like the one breath needed to break through and be present—but I'm more at ease with it, or perhaps I'm closer to the surface than I thought I was.

———

On our final evening as a group we are asked to write six things that we can't live without. We're told to cross two things out, then another two, then one more. The one thing that's left, this particular counselor explains, is the thing that we have left in life worth fighting for.

I'd written Frankie's name six times.

GRADUATION

By the end of our stay we've explored every possible topic to do with addiction—origins of addiction, sobriety maintenance, relapse—and for the last forty-eight hours there's a feeling of freedom, much like the last day of school when you feel like tearing through hallways and high-fiving even your most tight-assed teachers. Ours is a small class—there were more than twenty of us when we started; now we're down to eleven. Just like in high school, we get punished for smoking, and many people were kicked out for that.

The weather is fantastic. It's crazy-warm, summer-like. I make my only jeans into shorts; my roommate lends me a tank top.

We're allowed to stay outside for as long as we want, and all eleven of us spread all over the benches around the basketball court.

I watch families pushing old men and women in wheelchairs through the parking lot toward the seniors' unit.

Even though we're about to leave, people keep talking about being able to switch buildings, what it would be like to wake up facing the lake instead of a parking lot or a fence.

One of the counselors says that the building is a palliative-care unit. Someone makes a joke that so is ours, although it may take us longer to buy it, you just never know.

My roommate says that Donicio probably won't have to wait long at all, and he calls her a dumb whore and walks back into the building. She runs after him screaming his name in a shrill voice.

Sebastian, the guy who follows me around, takes off his shirt and flexes his biceps for me. Am I sexy? he says.

Very, very sexy, I say.

I can't wait to leave.

———

And then it's here.

We're leaving the next day. Now it's only ten of us left. Someone lost it the night before, went out and used. The day before graduation and he went out and used. It's the guy who supposedly liked me, Sebastian. I can't help but wonder if I was being too much of a bitch to him. But no, I know better than to give myself so much credit—nobody can make anybody use. Using is a personal decision.

When someone brings up the subject in our regular morning meeting after the tobacco propaganda, one of the counselors says that leaving right before it's time to leave is totally normal. But he won't say a lot more than that since the counselors are not allowed to discuss other clients. A late onset of relapse is a normal part of recovery, the counselor assures everyone.

Almost everything seems to be a normal part of recovery. Relapse, slip, overconfidence, compliance, happiness, unhappiness, hunger, loneliness, friendships, too much of something or not enough of something or just the right amount of everything—every single thing can be a normal part of recovery.

———

The next day, we leave as early as possible. It's dark outside, the day hasn't even started. Donicio is wearing a suit and nice shoes. The Priest is dressed in his usual black. Both of them light up as soon as they exit the building; they're standing and smoking, right in front of it. I find their urgent smoking defiant. But maybe I'm reading too much into it. Maybe they just wanted to smoke.

Sade is waiting with me in the lobby, in her pink PJs, a tiny, flimsy robe wrapped around her tightly. She's leaving later; one of her sugar daddies is picking her up. The same one who dropped her off. She looks worried, as if she had to stay another week instead of just a few hours more. She pokes her head outside, says something to Donicio, who says something back to her and she yells, Jerk!, and laughs, delighted.

Tina is talking to Kevin, still trying to exchange numbers with him, but all she gets is an email address. In a few hours she'll see her Scottish boyfriend, Douglas, and she won't have to think about Kevin, but I understand where she's coming from—anything at this point. Only hours separate us from re-entering our regular lives, but we've been thinking of leaving for the past three weeks so often that it seems that this waiting will never end. The last half-hour seems to stretch into infinity.

Finally, magically, the cab that will take us to the bus station in town is here. Sade screams and throws her arms around Tina, then me, then she runs out and kisses Donicio right on the mouth. She gives the Priest a big hug and almost kisses him on the mouth too but Kevin calls her name, like a teacher, and she rolls her eyes and goes back inside, shivering in her nightclothes.

That's my last image of New Hope: Sade with her too big doll-like head, full of bouncing curls, her arms crossed, vibrating, and her hands rubbing together for warmth.

———

On the bus, Donicio takes his jacket off. He's got a nice dress shirt underneath, clearly ironed. He must've had it hanging in the closet, ready for this final day, the whole time.

Donicio is already walking the streets in his clean, crisp shirt, running into his friends, doing his thing. This is what, I imagine, goes on inside him; the body on the bus is just delivering him there. He's not as talkative as usual; even his laughter seems restrained when the Priest tells us jokes.

Donicio exchanges phone numbers with Tina, says he'll give her a call for sure, once he's in the city. I can't imagine what they're going to do together. Go shopping?

The Priest passes us scraps of paper with his first name and an email address written on it. He doesn't have a phone, doesn't have an address yet. He's staying with Donicio for a week and then who knows. That's another thing about Donicio: he's invited the Priest to stay with him. I like Donicio quiet, and generous like that, different than he was inside. I know it will seem too out of character, maybe even like a capitulation, if I suggest exchanging numbers with him. I want to. But I don't and he doesn't ask and I feel a little hurt by that.

———

The men get off in St. Catharines. I've never been to St. Catharines before. In the darkness, the bus terminal seems more gray and more depressing than anything I've seen so far this morning.

Donicio says maybe he'll see me in meetings.

Maybe. But I doubt it.

You're funny, bella. Ciao.

Then it's just Tina and me and the rest of our trip. We don't talk to each other. I look out the window and it's the same blur of parking lots, warehouses, fences as it was on the way here.

———

Then I'm home. Standing right in front of my house.

I don't knock right away. Not yet. I stand on my tippytoes and look inside.

There he is, my boyfriend with his glasses on. I still never think of him as someone who wears glasses, so I'm startled again by this new incarnation. I notice he's maybe slouching a bit too, shoulders slightly more inward.

The baby is on the floor, playing. My boyfriend approaches him and the baby looks up. My boyfriend picks him up. The baby's face is turned toward the door but he can't see my face in the tiny window, he has no idea to look there for me.

I don't want to knock. Not yet.

I just want to watch them, love them from outside, keep them the way they are, undisturbed by the chaos that I bring with me. I miss them both so much, although the baby I miss beyond missing. It's like half of your face gone, your mouth and eyes.

———

I stand and watch them. I can't cry. But I want to.

———

When I can't take it anymore I knock on the door. It opens and then it's a blur of shouts and hugs and kisses and tears—theirs— and the only clear thing is the baby's weight against my body, which makes me feel immortal and, at the same time, completely disappointed that I am not.

AGAIN

Two months later, I'm drunk, again.

I don't understand.

The next day, my boyfriend is silent, cold. We don't talk. I don't remember. I hold a fist to my mouth to stop myself from vomiting. The vomit is pressing against every single pore in my body. I am so thirsty I would drink vinegar if it were offered to me.

I have to leave the house before I fall apart completely, so I pick myself up, put on a dress and walk into the hottest day in May in the history of the world. I walk and stop and retch, not so discreetly beside the stroller.

I surface. My monster slobbery face, eyes bleeding, looking at Frankie looking at me from the stroller. I'm trying to smile, trying to tell him that Mommy is really okay, sweetie, it's no big deal.

I also have the worst stomach cramps, so I have to run into various fast-food joints along the way. Once, I don't make it in time and a bead of something too liquid slides all the way down my legs. I wash the back of my dress and dispose of my underwear in a random bathroom stall.

These are the indignities of a chronic drunk.

———

I spend the rest of the morning sleeping in the park, sleeping off my hangover, the baby sleeping in the stroller.

I wake up with grass blades engraved in my face. There's a car parked nearby, a guy sitting in the car, watching.

I feel better after my nap. I let the baby out on the grass and he tries to push the stroller. He pulls my hat off my head and puts it on his. Now that I'm not feeling so sick, I am hungry, and we walk toward a park restaurant. I put the baby back in the stroller. He's babbling to himself and laughing. We lose my hat somewhere but that's okay.

After I eat, feeling slightly more human, I dial my boyfriend, desperate to tell him how much I love him. I need to see if things between us are okay despite what I don't remember happened the night before.

He answers the phone and I can tell he's mad but he says nothing about last night. We make small talk about what we're going to do later on. I can tell he wants to go but I'm scared I'll lose him. I am losing him already. I take a deep breath.

I tell him there was a scary guy watching us, just sitting in the car.

What scary guy? Are you okay? Do you need me to come and get you guys?

I exhale.

No, I think he's gone. I'm fine now.

He cares.

———

On my way back from the park I walk into a liquor store.

I don't even pretend that I'm *not* going to go inside. I just go inside. I don't make any stupid jokes or comments about having a big party or anything like that. They can all blow me if they have a problem with me drinking while caring for a baby.

I should go home and stick this wine and the vodka in the fridge, not even bother pretending that I didn't buy it. By now my boyfriend probably knows all of my hiding spots anyway.

A GIRL WALKS
INTO A SNAKE

A few weeks go by during which I put myself on a painful schedule of drinking only twice, three times a week tops. On the days off I stuff my schedule chock full of mommy-baby activities, visit galleries, draw, write novella-length emails, watch endless reality-TV shows. When I drink, I go back to my old routine of drinking after everybody goes to bed and passing out.

But unlike in the winter, it's harder to confine myself and my drinking to home, and I start to crave social interactions—places where I can showcase the extreme wit and charm that I sometimes believe myself to acquire after a gallon of booze. Nothing in my most recent history testifies in favor of this belief, but—perhaps because of the warm weather, the sense of renewal—I suddenly get the rock star feeling of being invincible, get back into that

Cosmo-woman fantasy that tells me that I do really well on booze. I'm sentimental too, like any drunk. For example, I'm still hanging on to one of my favorite memories of myself at twenty-one, wandering some city in Europe, in a blue dress, unwashed, drunk on vodka, hair full of sun and cigarettes, laughing with close friends who at night would turn into accidental lovers. We were going to live forever, of course, and we were always going to be drunk and it was always going to be summer.

———

Even after all my winter misery and rehab and sadness at home, this memory and all my other delusions are what seem to drive me. When the first summer invitation comes my way, I accept it immediately and convince my boyfriend that we should go.

On the day of the party, I'm walking toward the venue, a gallery, where I'm supposed to meet my boyfriend. I'm with the stroller and I'm wearing a tiny hat with feathers, and a blue silk dress. I look great. I'm bombed. Actually, I'm so bombed I can barely walk in these new stilettos, but holding on to the stroller supports my wobbling perfectly.

Hey, someone says behind me, I remember you.

I turn around. Someone familiar. Short, stocky, with round, happy cheeks.

Hey, it's me, Rob. The manly voice confuses me for a moment but then I remember. It's the AA lover from the harm reduction group. The one who reminded me of a middle-aged woman and who I'd nicknamed "Lesbian Man" to myself. I stifle laughter; it comes out as a loud snort.

He says, What? What is it?

Nothing, nothing, I giggle, How are you?

I'm great, I'm great! Lolita, right?

Not quite. His mixing up of my name stops dead the giggles. I hate it when people get my name mixed up with Lolita.

Jowita. Rob, right? Or Bob. Rob? Rob. It's Rob.

Rob.

Yes. How are you? Are you well?

I say, I'm great.

Great. Great. Where are you off to?

I wonder if he can smell it on me. I doubt it.

I smile, Oh, I'm just going to this party. Which is why I'm wearing the funny hat, see? I poke myself in the hat, say: See? See?

He finally looks, blushes and nods. Nice hat.

How's Jesus doing?

What?

You know, AA?

He blushes again.

I went to rehab, I tell him. It got worse. But now things are fine. Everything is so great.

Okay. Yeah, well, it's one day at a time, you know.

Oh, yeah I just love those slogans, love them—I squeak loudly enough for my son to squeak in response from his stroller.

It's okay, sweetie, I assure my son and try to aim for his head with my hand to pat it, it's okay.

Is this the famous Frankie?

I don't like him knowing Frankie's name. I wish I had lied about Frankie's name in those meetings. I wish I had called him something like Arturo or Hugo. Too late now, I guess.

How ya doing, big man? How are ya? Rob-Bob says to Frankie. How are ya, buddy?

Bob.

Rob.

Rob, right. I gotta go. I'm going to be late for my thing.

Keep well.

Yes.

Great. I wish you another twenty-four hours.

At first I can't figure out what he's talking about. Then I do. Twenty-four hours. Right. I have a couple of those if you add up the days in my scheduled week.

I smile at him. Rob.

He's just standing here.

I smile again. I'm starting to feel a little clearer.

He says, Oh, before I go . . . Do you know the story about the snake?

There's a tiny bit of a headache creeping into the back of my head.

I shake my head no. I should know better but I can't help myself. Someone says "story" and I'm all ears. I'm a sucker for stories. So I have to hear this stupid story.

Rob says, There was a little boy and he came across a rattlesnake. The snake said, "Please, little boy, can you take me across the river?" "No, snake. If I pick you up you will bite me and I will die." And the snake says, "No, I'd never bite you. Just take me across the river."

A group of friends of friends walks by. One of the girls recognizes me and gives me a little wave. I'm sure they're on the way to the gallery where the party is. Oh, how I wish I was walking with them instead of being stuck with this freak. But screw them. Screw this girl. I should own this situation and this freak. I wave back, but they've turned around already. Screw them.

Sorry?

He carried it right across the river. The rattlesnake.

I thought he wasn't going to do that.

Yes, but the snake promised him it wouldn't bite him.

Jesus fucking Christ.

Rob says, So the little boy walked all the way across the river, holding the snake to his chest. And right before he put it down on the ground, the rattlesnake turned and bit him in the chest. And the boy yelled, "Why did you do that? Now I will surely die!" The rattlesnake looked up at him, smiled and said, "You knew what I was when you picked me up."

Rob-Bob is blinking at me.

What? Oh. Right. He's done his story now. Wow, excellent, I tell him. I really have to go now.

It's good to see you.

You too. You too.

You know, it's like the snake.

What is?

Alcohol.

Of course. Just like the snake. Nice to see you.

It's great to see you. It's a great hat. God bless you.

I'm now half-sober. I think my walk improves, I can feel it strengthen and I don't even have to lean on the stroller so much. Frankie is babbling away inside it. I think I need another drink before I can face the cool crowd, the girl who waved and all those other friendly, non-alcoholic people. My boyfriend.

I think about cautionary tales, snakes, their heavy-handed meanings as I walk into a bar right next door to the gallery I'm going to.

GROUP WORK

fter rehab I kept getting phone calls to sign up for the follow-up group, or aftercare as the people who phone from the mental hospital call it. I like that name; it makes me think of us as precious flowers, addicts like orchids that need to be attended to even after their time in a glasshouse.

The next time someone calls to ask if I'm interested in going, I finally give in and tell the nice lady on the phone that I'll come to the upcoming meeting. This is shortly after running into Rob. Perhaps his snake story made some impression after all.

———

So here we go again. Two months after rehab, I'm at yet another addictions group, held in the same college-like building as the harm reduction group was before. It's even on the same floor, and when I walk up I'm greeting the familiar photographs of sunsets and forest fauna in the staircase. The room is different than before—much larger and on the east side of the building, so out the window you can see all the addicts hanging out on benches, smoking.

We go around in a circle. Naturally. Same thing. Bunch of fidgety losers. Thumb-twirlers and leg-twitchers. Addicts. This person lectures everyone, that one is lying, another one makes me want to scream with her passive sheep face.

Our new counselor is overweight with lots of curly hair. She looks like someone who should be running a children's TV show. She addresses everyone in the manner of a children's TV host, as if we were all living in a Muppet land. I never remember her name.

Once in a while if I feel particularly inspired I say something to stir the shit. Irritatingly so—and believe me, I am irritating myself—I bring up a lot of stuff I learned in the past, say things like: you can't modify your alcohol or drug use, minimize it or control it. I say that I know that only abstinence works. Moderation is bullshit.

There are a couple of people in the room who claim to practice moderation, so they look to the counselor to fight me on this and she kind of does. Or doesn't, really. She's probably used to my type. She's probably just humoring me. She tells me to keep an open mind.

That's a slogan in AA, did you know that? I ask her.

She says she didn't know that. She says it works for some people, moderation.

Okay, fine, I say.

A lot of people in this particular group know each other; there are lots of inside jokes going around. Some people have been coming here for more than a year, as the aftercare groups can go on for as long as there's interest. The long-timers know each other's histories, ask questions about each other's families. I don't interact much with the group itself. Perhaps part of me is jealous, even though I don't want to know them. This is so typical of me to feel this way, be jealous of something I don't want and dislike. In any case, eventually I stop trying to challenge the counselor and the moderation bullshitters. I run out of steam and show up at the group only to avoid my boyfriend's nagging.

When we go around and give reports on our well-being since the last time, I lie to the counselor, tell her I've been staying sober. I haven't been staying sober and have already abandoned my short-lived twice-thrice-a-week agenda.

I still have one rule right now, it's the only rule I still have and don't break: don't get drunk on the nights of these meetings. Which means that I'm plastered six nights out of seven. I don't even bother making excuses anymore, not to myself that is. I just go into the liquor store every day, walk in there like a wind-up toy, and pick up what I need.

Around the same time I join the aftercare, somebody from the New Hope center calls and asks me how I'm doing.

I tell her I relapsed. Again.

I'm sorry to hear that. But relapse—

Is a part of recovery. Yes, I know. I'm on my way to getting better, I suppose. I've really perfected that particular part of recovery.

Is there anything that we can do? Do you want to talk to your counselor?

Yes, because I really need another counselor in my life, I say.

Who did you work with here?

I can't remember who my official counselor was. Maybe the

woman who looked like a bird, the one who had wood plaques with words like *Believe* and *Faith* all over her office walls? Or maybe the idiot that made us tap our foreheads to get rid of cravings?

I don't know, I say.

Let me check. It was Brenda. According to our files your counselor was Brenda.

Never heard that name before. But, no, yeah, I don't think I need to talk to a counselor.

Do you have any comments for us?

Naturally. I always have comments. I say something vulgar and unnecessary about people—and I suppose I'm thinking of my former roommate—having sex all over the place and being distracting.

We were aware of that. The reality is that it's hard to control.

So you were kicking people out for smoking but humping was okay?

No, not at all. But there's only so much we can do. You can make an official complaint, of course.

Of course. That's okay. I tell the woman on the phone I'm attending the post-treatment group. I say I'm trying to stay sober.

That's excellent news.

I think how excellent news would be winning a free trip to Europe, but whatever, sure.

Anything we can do to help, she says. You can even come back for another term.

At this I laugh because that's the most absurd thing I've heard so far. But I thank her for her concern and promise to stay in touch.

I DRINK ALONE

can't remember how, but early that summer I finally negotiate hiring a babysitter in the evening. In the past, we'd hired a lovely Jamaican lady to look after Frankie sometimes, but since we moved to our new house we haven't had much luck finding someone to help us out. My boyfriend feels overwhelmed having to take care of the baby, and I'm getting more and more sick of being trapped in the house night after night. My sister helps here and there but she's still in school and it's hard for her to make the commitment.

After we finally find a regular sitter, we book her for a few nights a week. On those nights my boyfriend and I always leave the house. We almost always go out separately. I go out with the pretext of wanting to work on my writing and he goes out to get away from me, I'm sure.

When I go out, I don't talk to people. I go to bars. Just order drink after drink and when I decide that I'm starting to look suspicious I change bars. As usual, I'm paranoid about being arrested. I look at people and try to figure out if they're off-duty cops. I don't do anything to warrant arrest. I fall off the stool once and I break a glass a couple of times, but nothing to even get kicked out for.

I think back to rehab and Tina and other alcoholics. I assure myself I am nowhere near as bad as some of them. I remember Tina's stories: drinking on the plane while working, then being arrested on landing; being put on probation, taking stress leaves, not being allowed to fly anymore; drinking in the park while walking her Jack Russell in the morning, talking to street people, the dog earning the nickname Jack Daniels from the street people; passing out on a bench in the same park; Jack Daniels almost getting run over.

I also think about Charlotte, or whatever her name was, the teacher who was in love with Donicio. I recall her horror stories of driving drunk all the time and crashing.

Sade and her crack binges and her arm jerking and flinging itself forward.

Please.

I'm just having fun.

———

In moments of whatever leftover defiance I still harbor, I have a few ideas about what alcohol is supposedly aiding me with. With its help a tiny part of me is still convinced that I can again be the cosmopolitan woman I tried to be in Montreal. Louboutin-red, ambient techno, martinis.

Once I get to that perfect place where I'm sufficiently buzzed yet not too drunk, I will even be able to revert to my old charming self from many years ago. I will again be the girl with loose hands and lips searching for new kisses everywhere.

Back in my fantasies, I'm again the girl walking the streets swaying sexily, with sun in her luscious hair, getting stopped by men. I am the girl who is taken to Paris by a man who just wants to be around her, who will settle for just looking at her. Like him, in Paris, the men will look. Some will say *ma chérie, ma chérie* as I walk—swaying, again, always—through markets full of tomatoes straight from vines, and peaches.

With the right amount of alcohol I am a superwoman. I will jump from tall buildings, run like the wind, charm whomever I choose and perform all kinds of magic tricks: get ahead of any lineup, walk through glass, fight anyone, kill a car with my fists.

My seductive powers are so intense that not just men in Paris—entire rooms of the world will fall in love with me.

I get phone numbers, give out phone numbers.

Money flies. Not my money, yours.

I am invited to parties. Not just any parties. *The* parties.

I meet the coolest person: an owner of a boutique hotel; a writer with a fatwa over his head; a hip-hop star. We will become instant best friends and will get on the plane and fly to St. Barts for the New Year's Eve countdown on the yacht.

I'm just going to have one more pint. I'm almost there, just need one more tune-up and I'll be ready to go. While I wait for this thing to kick-start inside me, I go outside for a smoke. I do my best to ignore the soreness in my breasts swelling with milk, and the slightly bloated, familiar face that almost brushes against me as I pass the smudged mirror on my way out of this place called something like Dodo & Fiddle.

———

One night, early in the summer, I go to see a movie on my own, bring my own wine and drink it in a dark corner. The movie is about a woman who discovers that her child is not her own. I think. I'm not sure.

There's an actress in it who usually plays neurotic wives of mean men or fallen mistresses. In every movie, she's got kids or is about to lose kids. Or has lost kids. In this one we're not sure if there were kids, or rather, a kid, to begin with.

The actress has red hair and porcelain skin speckled with green freckles. She cries a lot and her tiny nose turns red at the tip when she does. She often takes long baths in movies, or it seems that way whenever I think of her past work.

I'm paranoid that the staff will be wearing night goggles looking for people videotaping the movie, finding me instead, guzzling wine from a box. Which is why I start drinking fast, gulping huge, sweet, sour and dank swigs to get rid of it for good. On the screen, the red-haired, red-nosed actress is drinking almost as fast out of a fancy glass of wine. I toast her in my mind as I finish up on this side of the screen.

Afterwards, the wine stays lodged somewhere in my throat. It wants to come out and spill all over my lap and the seats in front of me, even the screen. I talk to myself, calm myself down. Shh, it's just wine, you'll be okay. Shh, baby, I say, and think of my own baby and for some reason that makes me sort of cry—but not really cry, just pretend-cry. And I say—this time out loud, I can hear myself but pretend I can't, pretend this is completely involuntary—Be quiet, baby, shh.

From behind me someone says, Yeah, baby, shush the fuck up already.

I think about getting up and telling him to go fuck himself. But I'm too barfy.

So I try to make myself comfortable. On the screen the actress is sleeping in a bathtub. She looks dead and even more porcelain-like with water shining, accentuating the sharp cheekbones and, at the same time, softening her alabaster brow. It makes me tired just to look at her, so heavy-lidded and weak with fatigue.

I come to when someone starts shaking me.

Ma'am. Ma'am, please wake up.

She's a pudgy teenage girl with kind eyes. I look around to see who she's talking to but I'm the only one here.

Ma'am. She called me ma'am.

She looks at something on my shirt, her eyes stuck there a beat too long. I look down.

It's a little splash of purple. A little spit-up, which is what you call the not-quite vomit from baby's burp, as I have learned in my short career as a mother.

I'm sorry, I say to her, and she shrugs and says, That's okay. There's a washroom just outside if you need it.

Okay.

When I get up—slowly, even though the room is spinning, the now black movie screen tilting to the right—she reaches for my arm and then the empty box falls out of my lap.

She says, I'm so sorry, and squats to get it. But I'm faster than her, or I think I am, because I dive for the box with the grace of what in my mind is a bird of prey, but I move more like a fat turkey. I lose my balance and fall right on the girl. She tilts back and now she's falling too. This is a farce, a scene from an old black-and-white movie.

Now it's time for me to say sorry, again, and I will say it, I just have to get that stupid wine box out of her reach or out of her sight, so I kick it behind me. Then I try to help her up but she's too heavy or I'm too drunk or both. We go back and forth a few more seconds like this before we're both finally back on our feet. She's breathing loudly and her face is the same color as the stain on my shirt.

I leave the movie theater eventually, the empty box of wine squashed and shoved inside my pants. This makes me feel even dirtier than I already feel.

ONE

nside me, everything stalls. I begin to wish I was gone. For good.

I'm not being dramatic, just pragmatic. I feel that I'm wasting everyone's time, my own time especially. It's not that I've been destined to do greater things with my life—other than drink greatly—but now that I have this kid, I feel that I'm wasting my time pretending to be his mother.

I'm ruining my child.

I don't really want to commit suicide, but I start doing things like crossing the busy street two steps later than would be perfectly safe—my shadow getting struck and killed after I land on the sidewalk.

I stand too close to the yellow line on subway platforms, watching the trains approach, moving one step closer before they pull into the stations. I feel elated, nostalgic about my near-death when I get on. Elated because I didn't do it or because the option is always there next time, I can't tell.

At home, I casually google "painless suicide," "ways to kill yourself," I'm just a *researcher* of ways of death, I tell myself, but I store the information. I find that there's even a book called *The Complete Manual of Suicide* in which various methods are analyzed in detail. The book has graphs discussing every method (freezing, hanging, overdose, etc.) and it explores such important topics as the levels of pain, the preparation, and "the disturbance it may cause for others and its deadliness."

I also pray. I start praying one evening while in a liquor store, face to face with rows of bottles. It just comes over me, the prayer, like some kind of invisible blanket. It's desperate and quiet. It gets louder as I wrap my fingers around the box or the bottle and then there's nothing, just the hollow sounds of my trance as I pay for whatever I picked up. Outside, I come to again.

Sometimes, it's as if I am on a train going round and round, finally becoming aware of the fact that we haven't stopped at any stations in ages, and I start to wish for this, for the stop to happen. This is what I pray for. I need to stop. I need a stop, I need a stop, I need a stop, I chant in my head as I pick up bottles, and then drink them, later, after everyone goes to bed.

I have to stop.

Please give me a moment.

I can almost see it, this moment, like a ray of light from the sky, like some kind of cheesy religious image, a god's finger piercing glowingly through a cloud. I don't know. Whatever it is, I'm waiting for it because I need a break. Or I should just get on with it and die already.

I don't die but I finally finish my mat leave and in late May I go back to work. I'm back at my old job, the one I got while sober, long before I got pregnant. I think of all the jobs from my past—me sitting at various desks, in front of various computer screens, inhaling my own vapors from the night before. This was never the case in this job, but now it will be. Now I'll be sitting at my desk feeling as if my eyeballs were trying to fall out of my face. The alcohol will still be chasing itself through my veins and I'll be sitting at my desk, keeping my mouth, and every other hole, shut, to hold in everything that tries to escape the alcohol chasing inside my body.

I pretend to exist at work and make small talk and tell people stories about the baby. Everyone wants to hear about the baby.

I start smoking with the smoking crew and everyone seems a little shocked that I smoke.

I picked it up after I had the baby.

Really?

Yes, he made me smoke.

I try to make it sound like a joke. I succeed. I get laughs.

———

Mid-June, my boyfriend's mother comes to town to celebrate Frankie's first birthday. Her presence jerks me out of my overall numbness. I know she is watching me, I can tell. I try to tell myself I am being paranoid again, but what do you know—the second day of her visit she takes my boyfriend aside and tells him that she could smell vodka on my breath. I pretend to be indignant when he confronts me about it later, after dropping her off at her hotel.

Very funny, I tell him.

I don't know whom to believe, is all that he says.

I know that he doesn't believe me. I know that.

———

On the day of Frankie's birthday, I think about that first day in the hospital after he was born.

You were only a little baby, I say to his baby face. He looks at me with serious eyes.

He has no idea it's his birthday. How could he know? Still, I've bought him ridiculous amounts of toys—bags of colorful building blocks, trains, trucks. I already know that he'll be more interested in the packaging than whatever is inside, but I love the illusion of celebrating this milestone. I'm overcompensating.

My boyfriend is cold. I suspect he has reached his limits with me and his hate is slowly surfacing, getting harder and harder to hide. He gives me a murderous look when I joke about deserving some presents. I mean, it was mostly my doing that the little human is here with us and it was me who spent twenty-three hours in labor.

It is that look that upsets me and I decide that I'm not joking after all and we almost have a fight as I whine about not being appreciated. We make up because it is Frankie's birthday and we shouldn't be fighting. At least not in front of the baby, on his first birthday. Even if he has no idea it's his birthday.

He's looking at our faces—eyes still watchful, big—as they explode, implode and then quiet down.

Everything's okay, sweetie.

Are you sure? his eyes ask. He's in his high chair, eating cereal.

I'm totally sure, my eyes say back.

I have no idea what happens during the day. I guess I go to work. I pick up some vodka on the way home.

When I get home, my boyfriend's mother is already waiting for us to get ready. We're supposed to go to a fancy restaurant to celebrate the big event. The birthday.

My boyfriend's mother is nice to me but I imagine I notice her looking at me a little too closely. I wonder if I should bring up the vodka-smelling incident from the night before, but I decide to let it go. This is my method of convincing people that they're wrong about me—to show them that I have no qualms about attacking the issue head-on. I figure that they can't possibly think I'm guilty of something if I confront it myself. My delusional bravery is a substitute for honesty. But it's too risky to bring it up now, especially since there's not a lot of time left to get ready for our dinner and I still have to down my mickey.

I drink the mickey in the bathroom while I get ready. It goes down so easily lately, just drinking it straight from the bottle—no problem. I ignore the burning, just bear it, pretend I must do this. I must do this.

————

Maybe it's the presence of my boyfriend's mother downstairs, or just the general sense of urgency today, but I finish so quickly I'm suddenly panicked about not having had enough. This is always a problem. I never have enough. But I can usually just change places, move, pass out. Tonight is supposed to be many hours of being stuck at a restaurant table, pretending. I am no longer capable of just sitting. Just sitting is the most impossible thing. I can't imagine it happening.

I never know what I'm going to do. But now I worry. I worry that I know what I'm going to do. Just sit there and sit there. And sit there.

I do my eyes. I do something with my hair. Twist it and tie it—one mickey, what was I thinking?—and pin it.

I open the bottom drawer in the vanity. This is where we keep all the pills and Band-Aids and medical things like that. I know there's nothing illegal in there, no fun pills—I've eaten all the fun stuff already—but you never know and this is an emergency.

Noises from downstairs: baby giggling.

I open the door to the bathroom to announce I won't be much longer. My boyfriend says, okay, no rush.

I start sorting through various bottles and containers and boxes of crap in the drawer. Nothing. Just your regular Tylenol and vitamins and such. Finally, I fish out a bottle of sleeping pills. They are my boyfriend's prescription pills, so I guess they are better than nothing. I never take sleeping pills. I suppose they sort of make you high? They make you sleepy, too, I'm sure, but with my energy levels that'll be impossible. So maybe they'll just numb me out a bit more to get me to that perfect level. So that, for once, I'll be able to just sit.

———

Now we are in the restaurant and my boyfriend's mother is saying something. Everybody is saying something. I'm saying something. Or I think I'm saying something. But I can't open my mouth; it requires too much energy.

Speaking of energy, the restaurant is screaming, dishes are being broken somewhere in the kitchen. There's music playing over the noise, something with a steady beat. We're in the middle of the room, people are eating pasta out of bowls all around us. Everyone is so annoying, talking and laughing. Shut up. I'm so tired. Deadly tired. Tiredly dead.

The baby is smashing things, bread, throwing it on the floor.

The waiters say it's no big deal.

It's his birthday, I explain.

One of the waiters says to me, Happy birthday.

Not mine, I meant the baby's birthday. I'm not celebrating anything. I am, but it's *his* birthday. I'm celebrating the baby's birthday, right?

My boyfriend's mother looks at me.

I get up. I have to go to the bathroom, I announce.

I drag my feet up the carpeted stairs.

Why is there a carpet on the stairs? This is a restaurant, no? Carpet on the stairs, I say to some girl walking by, can you believe it?

In the bathroom, I lock myself in the stall and lay my head on my knees. Just a micro nap. No more than two minutes. How long could a person be in the bathroom to not be in there for too long? Ten minutes? How about a ten-minute nap, then.

People walk in. A bunch of women talking. There's only one other stall. Too bad.

It's nice and warm in here. I fall asleep for a moment.

There are more voices, closer, some at the door. Somebody says, I can see her feet.

Her feet. My feet.

I open my eyes. God. Please. Shut up.

Yeah, I can see a pair of heels. Hey, you okay in there?

Heels. I'm wearing a new pair of heels. I can hardly walk in them sober and in this condition it's a miracle that I've made it all the way up here. Probably because of that carpet on the stairs.

Another girl voice: You okay in there?

Yeah, yeah, I mumble. I'm gonna be out in a sec, just give me a sec.

I want to go back to my nap but it's probably a bad idea. I don't know what to do. I need a shock, I decide. I'd put my head in the toilet but I can't with all those stupid bitches outside.

I'll slap myself in the face.

First, I flush the toilet. Then I slap myself in the face. As hard as I can. I do it again and again. Flush, slap. Flush, slap. Wake up.

I'm not much more awake at all when I leave the stall.

I walk out of the bathroom and walk-cum-slide down the carpeted stairs back to the room where my boyfriend's mother is sitting by herself now.

They just went outside. Frankie's having a bit of a tantrum.

Okay.

I sit down.

I get on well with her, when I'm sober. She's a beautiful and stylish woman and I love her sense of humor. I admire her. I used to watch her play stupid when her husband was alive, watch her pretend to forget things, do Marilyn Monroe eyebrows, girly laughs. And then she would do something—make a comment, stifle a giggle—that would be exquisitely discreet but so telling of the big brain whirling in that girly head of hers. Her husband was officially the smart one, but I wasn't fooled.

She was slippery, clever. Which is what I remember now and it paralyzes me.

I may be drunk and three-quarters asleep but I'm in no way re-laxed. Just the opposite. I'm in the throes of the worst combination of panic and coma.

How are you? You seem a bit flushed, she says, and her eyes scan my face. They seem to stop on my mouth.

Okay. I'm okay. Just so tired. We didn't sleep much last night. Frankie kept getting up, wanting to be fed. I used up all the for-mula. I'm very, very tired.

You look tired, she says and lets it hang there as if waiting for me to say something. It's not safe to say anything else, so I'm quiet.

I think she knows anyway. I also wonder if my face is bearing red handprints.

My boyfriend comes back with the baby. I pull Frankie onto my lap so that the boyfriend can eat the dish that has just arrived. Frankie twists and tenses his little back and refuses to sit on my lap. My boyfriend's mother starts cooing to him, trying to distract him, but there's no distracting him.

I better get up and take him outside. To calm him down, I an-nounce.

Are you okay?

Of course. And to prove my point I walk as steadily as I can with a squirming baby and four-inch heels and with sleep that keeps pulling me under, not letting me off for a moment, even as I walk.

I sit outside on the steps with the baby in my lap, now quiet be-cause he's distracted by what's going on around us. The road is busy. On the sidewalk there are people walking by, women's eyes smiling at him, and everyone's waving to him the way they always do.

I bury my head in his shoulder, feel him lean into me. If he could only stay this way. Still and hot. I could sleep a little.

But no, he squirms. He's squirming so much I consider putting him down on the ground to teach him a lesson. See what happens. Someone stomping on him. Cars.

My boyfriend comes out of the restaurant and takes Frankie and says that I should go inside and eat.

His mother excuses herself when I show up.

I try to give her a smile but my mouth won't cooperate and I end up yawning instead.

Before I have a chance to fall face down in my plate, my boyfriend comes back with the baby. He says again that I should eat. He says this through clenched teeth.

I eat whatever's on the plate in front of me. I've no idea what's on the plate in front of me.

I order coffee. Another one.

I'm fine, just really, really tired, I insist. My boyfriend keeps asking what's wrong. His mother says nothing. Her mouth is getting thinner and thinner as the evening progresses.

The baby is trying to wiggle out of our arms again.

Well, are we done? says my boyfriend.

My boyfriend's mother snaps out of it and says chirpily, Let's get a dessert.

All three of us start waving at the waiter, desperate to not pay attention to one another if only for a brief moment.

The waiter comes and I tell him that it's the baby's first birthday.

He smiles and says nothing.

Perhaps I already told him that. I can't tell the waiters apart.

The dessert arrives and I dive in. Maybe the sugar will kick-start me. I try to give the baby a spoonful of crème brûlée, but he won't have any, moves his face away and spits.

My boyfriend's mother takes a picture.

The baby whacks the bowl of crème brûlée suddenly with his little fist and it shatters on the ground.

I shout.

The boyfriend shouts at me for shouting.

The waiters are here again, shouting that it's no big deal.

Let's just go, I say, and my boyfriend says something back and then I tell him to fuck off and his mother says loudly, Stop it you two, but I know she wants to say things loudly to me exclusively but won't because she's too polite for that.

They bring us our bill right away. My boyfriend's mother pays.

Outside we get into separate cabs. As soon as we start moving, I fall asleep with my head on my boyfriend's arm, the baby safely buckled up on his lap.

LOST AND FOUND

I don't know where I am. This place looks familiar but it also looks completely foreign, like a sketch of a place that I should know but the sketch is too wacky to make any sense of. This often happens when parts of my mind are still short-circuiting between a black-out and consciousness, trying to hang on to the latter.

I have my bicycle with me and I'm not wearing any shoes. I'm not in the middle of the road for a change, falling off my bicycle and breaking one of my shoes. That's what I remember doing just a few minutes or few hours ago. My baby's birthday was three nights ago and then I broke my shoes tonight, but that's all I recall at first. I'm now somewhere where I don't know where I am and it's been three days since my baby's birthday and I broke my shoes. That was tonight, the shoes.

Once I recall the shoes, there are suddenly more memory scraps of what unfolded this evening. First there was vodka at home, then I was on the patio of a bar, with a friend, and I fell off a chair. Then I had to go. I was thirsty. I ordered pints in another bar, a shot of something. Then I was falling onto the road, twice, cars swishing by, blaring their horns, massive bright lights right in my eyes.

———

Now it's not light at all. I'm more or less safe, I suppose, not lying in the middle of a speeding road with broken shoes, but I can't tell for sure. I'm too drunk to focus long enough to know what the what.

I'm so lost.

I have no choice but to call for help. I dig my cellphone out of my pocket, my hand reaching there as if on autopilot, some kind of a physical memory that tells it that's where the phone is. Me? I can't remember shit like that. I can't remember the number either so I try to punch it without looking, letting my fingers do the remembering.

Where are you? my boyfriend says.

I don't know. I don't have any shoes. I lost my shoes.

Are you okay?

I don't know. I'm not. Can you come and get me?

I can't. Everyone's gone home, I'm alone with Frankie.

Just leave him, he'll be fine.

Where are you?

I look around me again. I'm in another dimension, that's where I am. It's as if some force grabbed me when I was going into a blackout and then just threw me right in the middle of here, wherever here is. But I have to try to figure it out. I squint and look around. I move slowly with my cellphone, surveying the area. No clue. Sidewalk, glass, cars, vegetable stand. I don't know.

What do you see?

Sidewalk, glass, cars, vegetables.

What's the name of the street?

What street?

Just look up, what's the name of the street that you're on?

Look up. Okay. What does the street name look like? Can't remember. I remember that it should be on the corner, though, so I look toward what I think is the corner.

I have to walk up because my eyesight isn't so good without my glasses. Where are my stupid glasses? Shit.

Can you see it?

Clarens Avenue and Bloor, I read out loud. This sounds familiar. Am I here? I say.

Clarens Avenue and Bloor.

I lost my shoes. Come and get me, please.

You can walk, it's close. You're right around the corner.

No, I scream into the phone, but there's no one on the other end.

I can't walk. I have no shoes. But I walk.

———

The next morning it's the usual. I wake up in bed, terrified. Before I turn around to face my boyfriend—I hear him breathing behind me—I make up my mind about the course of action. I will not let him bully me. I can't remember much from the night before and I know for sure that I came home shoeless, but I don't remember anything after I started walking. So I don't even know if he saw me or not. I have to assume yes. And if yes, I better not let him bully me.

Or should I just apologize? Assume that bad things happened—they always do—and that I owe him an apology. Promise that I won't do it again. But do what again? I promise him I won't do it again all the time. I apologize all the time. Maybe I can think up a good story, something about how I lost my shoes because of a genuine accident, something about falling and having a concussion, something—

I can't do this anymore, he says behind me.

Even as I rise, sit up, and all kinds of defensive lies fall out of my mouth, I feel some kind of resignation, an obstacle inside me that wasn't there before.

I say things.

He says nothing else.

The baby cries in the other room.

———

I get up to attend to him and then I feel pain so sharp that it breaks me in two and I fall right beside the bed.

Are you okay? my boyfriend says. His voice is a sigh.

I don't think so.

I'm on the floor. I look down. My right leg is a mess. My left leg is a mess. The skin on my right knee is grazed down to a bloody jumble with pieces of black embedded in it, now throbbing loudly in pain. But it's not what has made me fall down.

It's the fucking little toe. The littlest toe of them all, which is now not so littlest at all but is instead a big fat cherry of a screaming—no, throbbing—ache. Ridiculous. A little toe.

I'll go check on him, my boyfriend says, meaning the baby.

I look closely at my little toe. I touch it but recoil immediately—it's as if I just poked myself with a hot needle—the sensation is so intense that I let out a loud moan.

My boyfriend comes in with the baby in his arms, the baby stretching, extending out his arms ready to fall into mine.

I say, I think I broke it.

Okay. My boyfriend passes me the baby, sits down on the edge of the bed.

I lie down on the bed with Frankie crawling all over me and making happy sounds.

I can't do this anymore. I think we should split up, my boyfriend says.

I had a concussion. I fell off—

No. No, you didn't. You were drunk. You came home without shoes. I can't do this anymore.

I got hit by a car.

You got hit by a car? You should see a doctor, then.

I need help.

I can't help you anymore. I don't want to help you anymore. I don't want to be with you anymore. I'm going to call the lawyer. If you want I can call one for you too. I'm going to look for a place or you can start looking for a place. I think you should probably start looking for a place right away.

I'm stunned. Every word falls on me like a brick. It's a shower of bricks. He says everything that I don't want to hear, can't bear to hear. He has a right to say all those things, to mean them.

It's over.

What lawyer? I don't know any lawyers. He has lawyer friends. His friend Tommy is a lawyer. Tommy's going to take his side, of course. They've been friends for years. Everyone, in fact, is going to take his side.

I've no one. I'm all by myself. The baby will be taken away. I'm a poor, stupid drunk slut, that's all. I'm nothing and I have nothing.

I think about all that but then I say something entirely different. I say hurtful, mean things and I make up lies, more lies. The more lies I say, the easier it'll be to believe them, I hope. I go back to the concussion story. It was a concussion, I insist.

Concussion, he says and gets up.

———

Slowly, painfully, I hop around the house and get myself and Frankie ready to go out. We'll go to a park, I'll have a little nap as usual. Frankie can sleep too. Yes, good. We'll sleep, we'll clear our heads, things will make more sense once we clear our heads. I'll be able to convince my boyfriend that what I'm telling him is the truth. Why does he suddenly refuse to play our game where he pretends to believe what I tell him even though we both know I'm lying?

I strap Frankie in the stroller and hop out of the house.

It's a beautiful day. I'm wearing white. I've washed my wounds and put dressing on my knee and on the smaller gash on my left leg. It's not pretty but at least it's clean. The white squares match the dress. I have a hard time walking but I figure out a way to place my left foot in a way—big-toe pad first—that there's no pressure on the stupid little toe.

I'm going to think about things today and then I'm going to go back home and convince my boyfriend of my innocence. I'm so sick of being accused. I can't take it anymore. This is really unacceptable. What right does he have to constantly monitor me like this? I mean, why is this any of his business? I had a concussion. How is that my fault. I'm going to turn—

Then there's silence.

My own voice in my own head just disappears. And once it disappears, there's an absolute, vast silence.

It stops all. It stops me.

It's not a moment per se. It's the invisible, non-existent pause between time's passing, one minute turning into the next one. It's so big that it contains everything else—around me and inside me.

I see me and I am looking back, looking for help.

And with that glimpse, everything crumbles.

I'm a liar.

I'm a liar and I can't afford to lie anymore.

I'm an alcoholic, I'm a liar and I've lied about everything.

There was no concussion.

I drank.

I drank and rode my bike and fell onto a busy street and broke my shoes. I got up and got back on my bike and then fell down again. Back onto the street. There were cars whooshing by, honking, people on the sidewalk stopping, asking: Is she okay? Are you okay? Is she okay? Are you okay? There was me kicking off my broken shoes. Walking barefoot through the streets with my mangled bike, walking into the darkness, coming out of the darkness, lost.

But I don't want to be lost anymore.

What am I hiding? There are bruises all over my body. Yellow, green, blue, red. I hide them underneath white clothes. I paint my blackened nails over with red. I get sick and flush to hide the sound, wash and scrub to hide the smell. There are bottles hidden all over the city.

What have I built this tower of secrets for?

I glance down. Out of the corner of my eye I see that Frankie turns around the way he always does when he senses me looking. It's our magical connection, mother and son. We feel each other.

It's okay, baby, I say, it's okay. We're okay.

I'm only minutes away from home.

It's okay, it's okay, I keep saying to Frankie, to myself, who knows to what.

I walk back, stumble back. I'm crying but this is good. I'm just washing shit out. There's so much shit inside me. I could cry for days. Months.

I'm feeling so incredibly relieved too. Yes, relieved. I don't have to do this anymore. I don't have to lie. I don't have to make up stupid stories about concussions. I don't have to conceal my tracks—bottles, bruises—pretend I don't know where they've come from. My purse's double lining will get stitched, there will be no need to hide anything in any lining anymore. Everything will be out in the open with me. I will never get caught because there will be nothing to catch me with or to catch me for. I will live like a normal human being.

When I get inside the house, my boyfriend doesn't want to hear it. He's heard it all before. He's heard it many times.

But you don't understand. This time it's different.

That's what you said last time.

———

But it *is* different. And it doesn't even matter that he doesn't believe me. *I* wouldn't believe me. Who would?

I suppose I'm sad that he doesn't believe me, but I understand. I understand and I'm happy regardless. Frankie is here. As long as there is Frankie, I could be happy. I could lose my boyfriend, lose this house, our life as a family unit . . . and I would be happy anyway. Because this is over. Although it's not over for a fact—you can never know for a fact. I just know *right now* that it's over.

THE MOMENT

So now that I've finally caught *the* moment, stopped time and got out, I don't know any better how to catch it. Because, no matter what anyone tells you, stopping is impossible if you're a real addict. If you're an addict it's not in your nature to stop. It's in your nature to do more and more. And more. And more.

And how do I know that this is the magical moment? Why would *this* be it, why *right now*?

It's not fear of losing what I have, not my boyfriend's words and the consequences he has outlined. Because I know that I can probably go back and throw another lie at him, I can probably even reheat the concussion story and he will eventually capitulate and everything will go back to what it was like until one of us dies or something. Either way, we'll be miserable until forever.

I don't know for sure if this is the magical moment. But I know that right after I get back home to confess to my boyfriend and right after he rejects my confession, I don't crumble. I feel more solid than I have in months. Years.

And, limping on my broken toe, I march all the way across town to an AA meeting. Because that is the only thing that kept me stopped before. And this time I mean it. I really want it. I want it. The wanting is as strong as always. But now it's for the right thing.

THIS PART OF THE STORY

I f you've read other addiction memoirs, you know that this is the part where I talk about how difficult but wonderful things became after I got sober. Things got very difficult indeed after I got sober. The reality is that often I'm not sure if they got anything else. I'm not sure if they really got that wonderful and, really, what this wonderful is supposed to be.

In fact, it is wonderful that possibly makes me relapse. I'm always chasing it because I don't experience it—the wonderful—unless I'm truly on the edge. I understand the concept of wonderful, the concept of happiness, but I never feel as close to it as I do when intoxicated.

I know that here is roughly the part where I'm supposed to write that I found true happiness only after getting sober, but this is not the case.

I'm certainly feeling healthier already. But like the uncatchable moment of clarity in the midst of addiction, happiness is a glimpse, a flash going off. As an addict I see it—happiness—differently, or rather, I want to see it differently. I want to see it as a platform, a way of going even further, beyond happy. Fuck happy. I want ecstatic, euphoric. I want godly. Meeting my son for the first time when I gave birth gave me a surge of godly. But it didn't last long enough.

And, of course, I wanted more.

———

And now I *want* more again. And now I'm sober. The first time I got sober, it was the same: I wanted it more than anything. Now I *want* it again, just as hard. Yes, I wanted to be sober the whole time up until now but now it is desperate. The last ditch effort to jump off a speeding train. I don't have a solution or the answer of why now, why this way. It just is this way. This is no self-help book.

———

As for the meetings, I could go to one or I could go to a hundred but without desperately *wanting* sobriety, it wouldn't work. I need meetings to stay wanting, to remind myself how badly I *want* it, to see how there are others like me who want it just as badly. How there are many who want it but for whom the train of compulsion doesn't seem to stop. They never get that moment, that pause that will be long enough for them to get off. Because that's all it is—for some the train is too fast, some sleep through the stops, some jump off and jump right back on because they forget immediately that this is a death train. Me? I slept, went too fast, forgot . . . but then finally, stopped, limping on my broken toe, the lies falling off of me, making me light, making me vulnerable. Making me strong. So strong that for one moment I could halt the whole fucking train.

———

Once sober, I have to move out. Despite my breakthrough and finding the moment that lets me get off the crazy train and not have the compulsion to self-annihilate, I still have to deal with my situation. The situation is that I no longer have the comfort of my boyfriend's support. My sister is in England for the summer. And the mental-health workers, the counselors, have been abandoned over the months and it would be too inauthentic to rely on them now. Besides, I never really bought it, any of those therapies.

At home no amount of promises or screaming will persuade my boyfriend to let me stay. And part of me prays and hopes that he won't crumble. I have to act out despair and tears—which come too easily now—but I'm not convinced myself that staying home and being forgiven is what's best for me right now. So I shout and plead but in spurts rather than making this a continuous campaign. I'm sick of myself.

I'm sick of this, he says.

———

A few days later I go to the emergency ward with my baby for company. I am there to see someone about my broken toe. As I wait I think about how I used to come to the same emergency years ago to score some Ativan. How they make you take it in the room with them and they only give you two maximum because they've been trained to see right through the likes of you.

How I came here not that long ago, while still sober, and watched a cocaine addict sobering up from his latest binge. I saw him suddenly writhing in pain as his numbed nerve endings woke up. He screamed about the huge red-and-yellow pus-filled gash in his leg. He screamed back at his own leg and kept screaming and the emergency workers told him that they wouldn't deal with him if he was still high. The man kept screaming that this was precisely the problem—he wasn't high—and he screamingly demanded a wheelchair but they wouldn't bring it to him so he made himself fall down on the floor and then crawled through the revolving door into the emergency room, still screaming.

Sitting in the waiting room, I cry the whole time. I keep washing all the madness out. I enjoy it, almost. The nurses and other patients walk by and look at me and at the stroller and smile a sad smile. This is what it is going to be like, I think. People are going to smile. I'm going to be a single mother from now on, crying, dragging my child everywhere with me.

Briefly, I get excited by the concept of single motherhood, even though it's supposed to be challenging, but at least, for me, it's slightly closer to the edge that I wish to live on. I can't think of cokeheads crawling on the floor with pus and blood dragging behind them in a snotty trail right now. Forget it. But I could be a single mom. This could be interesting, running to pick him up from babysitters, cooking Kraft easy dinners, saying to potential dates: my kid.

Will I have to start stripping to support myself and my child? Will my C-section scar show when I shave off pubic hair to dance?

I don't take myself so seriously that I completely believe myself worrying about scars and stripping. I am so used to me. But this is the state of an addict's mind. It's a fantasyland. I sit in the waiting room, the sleeping baby in my lap, my ass about to be homeless, and I pretend to worry about the swollen cherry of a little toe and how I'm going to fit it into a Lucite heel.

———

I don't become a stripper. Since I have a job already I go to my quiet job as I do every day, although now I leave for it from another part of the city.

After I get back from emergency, the same night I pack my bags. Nobody is running after me as I leave and hop into a cab with a bag, first loading the folded stroller, the pack'n'fold crib. I come back to get Frankie. He's not getting kicked out but I've begged my boyfriend to let me take him that first night and he agreed. I'm staying with a friend, Cara, who's going through a breakup. Frankie and I set up camp in Cara's apartment above a restaurant that she owns. I unfold Frankie's pack'n'fold. Cara holds Frankie, who is quiet but sad. He's unsure of the new place. He looks around with big brown eyes.

Cara lives with a dog, a whip of a whippet that runs around on tiny nails and barks excitedly as I unpack my suitcase. Frankie's face crumples at this so I leave the unpacking and pick him up and make my voice as soft as possible, softer than the sleep-sheep toy he cuddles every night: It's okay, baby, it's okay.

I can unpack later.

I fall asleep with my face against the mesh of the pack'n'fold, breathing in my baby's breath.

I sleep on a beautiful vintage chaise longue with the window looking out onto a busy street, and across it a butcher shop with neon signs—*Lamb*, *Pork*, *Veal*, *Chicken*—always flashing, all night long, a carnivorous Vegas.

UP THE HILL

He waddles from me to my boyfriend and his face, like his steps, is hesitant. His chubby feet are flapping against wooden floors as he goes back and forth, unsteadily, holding on to the bed frame and the dresser. I'm sitting on the bed in our bedroom and I'm screaming. My boyfriend is standing in the corner of the room and he's screaming for me to stop screaming.

Frankie moves forward and lands against the bed, fat hand grabbing my thigh. I lift him up without looking at him because I'm too busy being angry. My boyfriend shouts to be careful with the baby. He shouts we have to stop shouting because we're scaring the baby. I shout to get used to this shouting because that's what things are going to be like from now on, shouty. On second thought, perhaps things won't be like this at all because we won't be around, me and the baby. Maybe he can go back to being a partying middle-aged bachelor, which is what he was when I met him. Maybe he can go and snort lines of cocaine off of women's asses and breasts as he always jokes about doing. Maybe he can find another stupid, naive student like me and fuck her and make her a baby and install her in this house to replace me. Us. Replace us. Because we're replaceable. Because we're not going to stick around much longer for this kind of bullshit.

Immediately, I imagine myself on the plane going somewhere warmer, nicer. Me and Frankie in a little apartment, then later, Frankie older, bigger, in some sunlit sandbox, maybe even a beach.

My boyfriend yells back that I can just go and fuck myself. I have no right to take him, the baby. Leave the baby alone. He's not a toy I can just take whenever I please.

Then in a normal voice he says the stuff about calling family lawyers again, which is what made me start screaming in the first place.

It's now ten days or so since I moved out. My newly found sobriety is coming out in big, angry, shouty chunks.

Frankie stops wobbling around and now sits quietly in my lap despite all the screaming. It occurs to me that maybe he's so quiet because of it. I have an old memory of running from one set of knees to another, just like him, a bouncy ball of a child's body between my parents, who tried to kill each other above me. I was older than Frankie is now because I remember telling them to stop it, to please be quiet. They finally stop and turn on me, telling me to shut up, but I don't. I keep shouting because I'm just buzzed from all this angry energy above me; I am hysterical and can't stop shouting to *stop it* myself, and then my cheek stings as someone slaps me. I stop it.

Is that what we're going to end up like?

The warm, heavy body of my son is against my body. There are anger and tears above him. How much I've messed up already. All I wanted to do when we were shouting minutes ago was to stop my son's little pattering around. Now that he has stopped I feel guilty and helpless because I can't think of what to do to make him happy.

Fine, lawyers, fine, I say to my boyfriend. Whatever you want.

I know he has contacted his friend Tommy already and I'm starting to feel the first elbowing of social disapproval, like when Tommy's wife sends a polite but cold email saying she's too busy when I ask her if she could meet with me. I don't really want to meet with her but I want the world to believe me when I say that I'm done drinking.

The world has no reason to believe me. I kept lying to it over and over.

Once we are quiet, I get up to leave. I don't want to fight. Or I want to fight but it is me I want to fight against. It's the past, the time before drinking, that I want to fight for. I want us to be a family again. I don't want to say any more hurtful things to my boyfriend. He is the love of my life, I remind myself, but this reminder makes me so ashamed that I can now only feel grief. I've broken us, buried us, and I can't do anything anymore to dig us up again and make it whole.

———

In the weeks that I'm staying at Cara's, my boyfriend and I divide custody of Frankie. After I drop Frankie off at the daycare or on the days when his father takes care of him, I ride my bicycle. I ride up the hills and down, for miles, pedaling and breathing loudly as I go up, letting my body sweat it all out as I go down.

My bike is barely holding together, still bent and twisted in places from my accident, but even that makes my excursion some-what more satisfying, its brokenness a testimony to where we've both been. The fact that I'm still riding it meaning we're better now.

I like feeling my muscles again. Since going to the gym at rehab, I haven't been this close with my own body's working. It's good to feel it again. I even like the pain in my lungs and the awful city dirt and dust that lands on me in the sweaty evenings and clings to me during hazy mornings. I don't mind at all.

I ride to and from work, and to and from my meetings. I fill up every free hour with going to and being at meetings.

On my days with Frankie I bring him to meetings. I know I'm becoming one of those moms with a writhing toddler who stands in the back of the room and leaves before the tantrum is in full swing but not soon enough to save everybody from a loud sample of tod-dler rage. Long time ago before I was a mom and before I relapsed, I used to get annoyed by these women in meetings. I remember hav-ing to talk myself out of the desire to shush them. I had to sit there, frozen in annoyance, and I had to keep reminding myself that they had no choice, they had to bring babies with them. And now I will be one of them and I'll have to put up with tut-tutting bitches like myself.

———

Three weeks after I last drank, I'm at a meeting and I go up with Frankie on my hip, to pick up a chip that stands for wanting to quit drinking. It's called a desire chip. I have to march across a room full of people to get it and I know from before that they will all clap madly when I walk back to my spot. This is the part I used to hate, but this time when I walk back and everyone claps, I feel touched and even a little proud of myself. Frankie loves when people clap, so he joins in, clapping his chubby little hands, after we sit down and honor the following thirty-day, two-month, six-month and nine-month chips that honor periods of sobriety.

Outside the windows, the trees are thick with green leaves. Like most meetings, this one is held in a room in a church building. It smells of cheap coffee and it's a familiar smell; I welcome it.

I don't leave this meeting early and there are no tantrums. We stay inside for the duration. Cara and her friend Kate take Frankie out near the end, when he fusses, and play with him as I sit inside the room where the actual meeting is held. I listen to a famous film director talk about binge drinking and smoking crack with bikers.

After the speaker is done talking, I go to find Frankie and Cara and Kate. They are in a classroom in the back of the church. Montessori classes are held here during the week, and my friends are playing with Frankie by the shelf filled with wooden toys.

He squeals when he sees me and triumphantly raises one arm to show me a piece of wood he's holding on to. Cara and Kate turn around and squeal too. They're squealing over the fact that Frankie is walking; they say he has made a couple of steady steps completely on his own.

Looking at the three of them sitting on the floor with open faces and big smiles, looking at my son with his cloud of golden hair and his face, his ruby-red lips and happy cheeks, and all that green August outside the window, and everything that makes this moment *this* moment—the smell of coffee still lingering in the air—I finally feel that we're safe and that things will be okay.

————

When I go home that night to drop off my son, my boyfriend is waiting for me and we talk. He speaks softly; his face doesn't twitch in annoyance. I wonder if he, too, had noticed how green and promising everything looks outside, if the evening summer light had made him feel something other than despair about us. If it had caused him to snap out of it, even feel some hint of hope.

We don't shout, don't say mean things to one another, just talk. Our voices are treading carefully, back and forth on this fragile golden line of cautious connection. We must be gentle with each other. We've been gravely wounded in this war. One more battle and there will be no returning.

I want to move back in, I say as I've said, threatened, begged many times over the past three weeks. Except that now I just say it, as strongly and as calmly as I can.

I don't want you to live here, he says the words that he has shouted and hissed before. Now he sounds resigned.

Just a trial. I will move back out if you want me to.

He says nothing.

Please, I say.

That's all I say. I don't talk about my drinking or how admirably sober I am. It hasn't been that long at all. There's no sobriety to talk about, really. But: Please.

A long silence. We used to be comfortable being silent with each other before silences became weapons in our war: Him not speaking to me the day after he'd catch me drinking. Me not speaking when I was too drunk to talk. But this silence is okay. I don't know if he's comfortable with it right now, but I am. I can sit in it. I'm not alarmed by it.

Okay, he finally says, just a trial.

Like a probation.

Okay. A probation. You have till the end of the month.

I can feel my heart flutter a little harder in my chest. I want to put my arms around him. I want to kiss him, feel his hard body against my soft one. My desire is physical but it also feels enhanced, as if there is a spiritual element to it, a need for a communion. But I can't break through his hate, have no right to expect anything from him yet, have zero proof that he, too, is feeling that hope, light, filtering through the trees outside that's letting itself inside. So I stand where I am.

I love you, I say.

He says nothing.

Thank you.

You're welcome.

I don't lose my respect for him for finally relenting. I think that he's brave and loving and that this, letting me move back in, has nothing to do with him being weak. He's in fact stronger than if he were to kick me out, because he's willing to take the risk. He is kinder than he is angrier. And that makes him a superior human being, at least superior to me. Me? I'm ashamed of everything, again, for having to put him in this position, but I'm also grateful that I've been given another chance. I have no clue if I will pass the test—I want to pass the test but my *want* is not the most reliable, it is not a fact. No matter. In the end I'm going to give it my best shot.

The probation starts the next day.

WEDNESDAY

'm an addict. There's no way to know what I will do. Most of the time I don't know what to expect from myself. I have lots of evidence that proves this.

While drinking, in the morning, on waking up, remorse already eating away at me like rot, I would beg. I would beg and plead for a good day. I would promise my god, your god, the gods of worlds, and all the godless world that I would not drink.

I would be drunk by the end of the day.

This is why I don't know the end.

————

Before we get to the end, I need to tell you about how I stay stopped.

Wednesday.

I do the same thing every Wednesday after work. I pick up my son from his daycare, first. I usually ride my bike, unless it rains. Same bike. Except this time around I've added a baby seat onto its back. I adorned it with flashing lights and I bought helmets for the kid and myself. I took it to the bike shop to tune it up. It still squeaks and coughs as I pedal, but at least now it sounds less like a death rattle.

I love picking my son up from the daycare.

He runs up to the gate with his little arms extended, pushing through other children and shouting, Momma mama mommy mommy-mommy. It's the best thing that happens to me every day, that shouting. It's the best thing. Ever.

And the face that comes with it—the smile of joy so authentic and absolute that most humans can understand and recognize it for what it is: god.

When I pick him up and he leans his curly head against my chest, sometimes it feels like too much love and I worry that I'll lose my balance and fall, sink under for a split moment, but then I always push myself through, all the way up to the surface. Nose to the blue horizon.

I can handle it. I can handle it now.

I get him dressed and strap him into his seat and put a helmet on his head. I knock on his helmet and then on mine and make googly eyes when I do. This makes him laugh. He dislikes the helmet but the googly eyes and the knocking distract him sometimes and he forgets to get upset.

Then we bike home.

We bike on a golden street with a pink and purple sky ahead of us. In the summer the street smells of sun and leaves; I ride the bike through a curtain of green parting against fences on both sides. It's a Hollywood PG-rated movie. (In the winter, there will be the raspy throat of cold and sharpness and shadows but also lamps turned on inside houses filled with families. Christmas magic in the air—the smell of pine everywhere.)

We pass a convenience store called Rosie's Garden. It's run by a Trinidadian woman, set up in old-school style with tables and chairs outside. She sells soursop ice cream, patties, sodas in bottles. You can sit and have your soda and ice cream outside when it's warm. This is where my boyfriend and I would meet when we briefly lived separately. It's where Frankie had his first ice cream ever. And my boyfriend showed up and joked about me trying the world-old trick of bribing my kid with sweets.

I laughed then but every time I bike by, I remember hating every second of our strange child handovers. On the Rosie's Garden patio, I passed Frankie over to my boyfriend and then rode off on my bike crying. Were we going to have to live through the weirdness of split custody from now on? Would any of us ever get used to it? The idea of being used to it only made me cry harder.

But now with Frankie on the back of my bike, those thoughts of what happened here early in the summer are only that—thoughts. The reality is that we're going home and that we're going to have a meal as a whole family tonight. As we do almost every night.

And after the meal, and after I kiss my warm pink little boy goodbye and leave him with his dad, I will go to where I usually go every Wednesday evening. Even today. I'm under the weather today and there's nothing I want more right now than to just hang out with my toddler, but I go. I go to my meeting. It's important.

Sometimes I believe that my life does depend on it.

So that's how I stay stopped.

SADE

It's September now and Sade's taller than I remember her. Thinner too.

She bounces as she walks and laughs as soon as she sees me. Then she stops a woman walking, demands she take our picture. Sade hasn't figured out her telephone's camera settings—it's a new phone—and I can tell that the woman is irritated by the request. They're both looking all over the oblong pink rock trying to find the button that will snap a photo. The woman finally shakes her head and says she really has to go, she'll be late for work, and that's when Sade shouts, Got it! Yes!

She wraps her arms around me and says, Say cheese, and the woman takes the picture or pretends to. Either way, she starts running as soon as Sade's got the phone back in her hands. Sade says something about people being unfriendly in big cities.

We look for a place to eat and decide on a small front patio of a French restaurant. As soon as we sit down, Sade says that her fucking ex, John, now has full custody of her boy but that she's getting him back. First, she has to go to South America with her new boyfriend.

She lights a cigarette and says, But he's not the guy I'm in town with. This trip is just business, and the bird wanted to act all boyfriend-girlfriend–like and I was like watch yourself, keep your hands to yourself, you know?

The guy, not the boyfriend, has paid for three nights and a hotel. He is at least sixty, she thinks, and kinda disgusts her. But it's good money. Not that good. Okay, it's okay.

Her phone makes a sound. She looks at it. She says, And then my landlord, he's helping me find some lawyers but I'm getting worried because he's all talk and no action. The fireman totally blew me off, by the way. Fucking bird. Just went off and disappeared. Oh yeah, that reminds me. Remember Donicio?

Who?

The guy I was fooling around with? Him and I talked a coupla times.

She presses some buttons on the phone, shakes her head.

Of course. Donicio. Like everything and everyone from that time, Donicio seems nothing more than some kind of cartoon character from my past. Sade tells me they met shortly after rehab was over, and they slept together. It was great, she says. They stayed in touch. Called each other a lot. They were making more plans to meet.

She says he talked to her a lot about the program. The AA program. He said he was going to meetings. He even talked her out of using once or twice. He was all gung-ho about keeping clean. But then he stopped calling.

Sade kept leaving him messages.

Donicio is not stupid. He does well for himself, Sade says.

He told her in the past he owned a used crane. He would rent it out to builders. He had to sell this crane to pay back his debts and fuel his habit. Heroin.

Sade nods, ringlets bouncing all over her head. Yeah, a whole crane. How much is that? Quarter, half a million bucks?

When she called him the last time, the number was disconnected, she says.

A waiter approaches our table. He's bitchy, with piercings in his nose and lip. He pretends to have a French accent. Sade laughs when he corrects her pronunciation of *niçoise*.

Hold the eggs, please, she says, and his face freezes and he tries to kill her with his stare, but she's not looking up. She's digging in her purse. Her phone is making squeaky noises again.

I ask for a *croque monsieur*. It's one of the five things I know how to say. But I guess I don't say it properly because the bitchy waiter says something in French that sounds like a question. Sade looks up at him then and says, She wants the ham and cheese sandwich for fuck's sake.

He'll spit in my sandwich, you know that? I say after he stiffly walks away.

Well, *he* would anyway. She lights a cigarette and asks me how everything is. Am I staying sober.

Yes.

Good for you. Good for you, I'm so proud of you, she says, and she does sound sincere so I ask if she's sober. Clean, I mean.

It's so good to see you, Sade says.

You too. (So she's not. Clean.) It is, I say. But it's strange to see Sade here outside of rehab. We're not far from where I work and I think about that. I think about one of my co-workers walking by and seeing me here with this beautiful girl and asking how we met and how I could say, Rehab. She's a crack whore, actually, I could add. Watch them slink away.

Our food arrives and Sade starts on her salad. She sets the lit cigarette in the ashtray. The smoke drifts, breaks into a curl that unties near her head. The waiter is silent, gives me a frosty smile when I look up as he sets down my plate.

I don't eat bread, remember? Sade says when I offer her a bite of my sandwich. I imagine a dollop of phlegm inside my sandwich. I hope she'll take the bite with the phlegm, in a lucky coincidence.

Not even a tiny bite?

She pushes my sandwich away.

But you're so thin.

Yeah, thin. Tell that to my pot-belly. It's all carbs. I look four months pregnant. And it's not good for you anyways. She picks up and waves her cigarette and rolls her eyes. Yup, carbs will kill you. She bursts out laughing.

After a couple of bites, the imaginary phlegm is too much to ignore. I can't finish eating. I grab one of Sade's cigarettes and light it.

Bonne petite, she laughs.

She talks non-stop the way she always does and I get lost in the sea of men, custody battles and bar fights. There are a few small crack binges in there too, something about the South American boyfriend doing blasts and wanting to have a foursome. She says she smokes only occasionally. Almost never. Like, once in a blue moon. She's off the stuff practically.

I want to believe her. I want to ignore that she keeps on laughing and her eyes say something else to mine, as if some version of our other, real selves were the actual ones communicating and telling it like it is. But maybe I'm imagining things.

I'm an addict. She's an addict. There's everybody, and there's us. We are reverse. Or upside down. Or who cares. Because maybe not. Maybe there's nothing special about us, addicts. We're tragic, but not special. Maybe we're just weak. Maybe I'm weak. Maybe I should stop being such a cunt and just believe Sade. Because I really want to.

She goes on about buying a car, her sister doing well on methadone. And Donicio being such a bird. She says, We were talking all the time and then I find out he's talking to what's-her-face, the teacher who was driving drunk. And she was giving him a hard time about me. And now I can't even get a hold of him? Hello? I don't need that shit.

The only time Sade's constant smile tightens a little is when she talks about John and her little boy. Fucking John.

I want to ask how he's doing, her boy. I half remember some story about Jamal putting some toy together or something and I try to recall the details but I can't. I want to ask her about it, to steer her away from all this pent-up grief she's got going on about John. But it's impossible. She goes on about how it's weird he's pretending to be all interested in the kid suddenly. He wants to be the perfect babydaddy. He's all up in her shit over how long she wants to keep the kid or if she's keeping him overnight. He's her kid for fuck's sake.

I steal a quick look at the clock inside the restaurant. I can't make out the exact time but I just tell myself that I've only got ten minutes left. I have a lot of freedom at work and can make my own hours within reasonable limits. But Sade doesn't know that. I mumble something about my lunch almost being over.

Oh my god, I forgot. You've got to go back to work. What do you do there? How's it going at work? I didn't even ask you. I always do this, think that I'm conversating with someone but it's just me talking. Wait, listen. We should meet tomorrow. No, wait, tomorrow I've got a date. But maybe later on this month? Maybe we could even go to a meeting. I used to go but I stopped, I'd love to go again.

Okay.

Great. I'll text you when I get the car and I'll take the kid and we'll come down. Maybe we can go to the zoo. And the meeting.

Sounds great.

I say it but I don't mean it. Going to the meeting with her. Or I do mean it but I already know that she's not going to follow through. There's a strange barrier between us, an invisible kind of thing. I don't know if it's me or her or just because we're not me and her anymore. We're in the outside world. So we're somebody else, some other two women. We're reverse and we're both addicts but we don't know each other.

Before we part, she takes a few more pictures of me with her phone. She's still not sure that the pictures are saving correctly but she waves it off. Next, she runs inside and comes out shouting that we're all paid up.

You didn't have to.

Do I know how much money she has on her? No? Then I should

shut the fuck up. And, she adds, you don't have to deal with that bird. She means the waiter.

This makes me laugh.

We hug.

I breathe in her scent. I do this sometimes, to recall or remember better. She smells of candy and cigarettes, exactly as before.

SOBER

On the subway, standing, I say excuse me, and a drunken man tries to stop me. He says that I need to go back to my own country. I can't hear my accent. I'm always surprised when people tell me I have one.

A male voice behind me says, Hey now.

It's okay, I say to the voice behind me.

The drunken man points to himself and announces that this is his country. He says, I'm Native American, pure blood, and this is my people's land. This is my country.

Silly drunken Indian, I think. You can have your country, I'm glad I'm not from your country.

And today is my birthday, he hollers. It's September twenty-sixth and it's my birthday.

Fuck your birthday too.

He tries to high-five a little black kid, You and me. We know what it's like—he keeps saying to the kid, who looks scared—we know what it's like to be with the whiteys.

I wish I could stop listening to this and just ignore it. Everything inside me wants to shout at this man, tell him what a sad loser he is. And I'm angry at myself for having the thoughts I'm having. I'm a racist piece of shit, fine. But this man, seriously. This stupid loser man.

He's finally walking away from me, pushing through people, still screaming about whiteys and about his people's land. I wish for him to trip, for the subway to stop abruptly to make it so. Then it occurs to me that the drunken Indian and me—whitey—we just may be from the same country after all, no matter what either of us says. And I don't hate him so much anymore.

———

When I get to the meeting, I run into Chris. Chris is with Cara. I remember now that Cara used to be Chris's sponsor, a kind of mentor that people in AA have to hook up with to guide them through the twelve-step stuff. I haven't seen Chris in more than a year. I haven't seen her since our photo shoot. She looks great. I'm surprised she looks great because of what I've heard. An almost-overdose, some crazy boyfriend who'd beat her up.

We greet each other nervously, her giant green eyes flashing from underneath heavy bangs. I have a little bit of a cold so I say to both her and Cara that I can't hug. Fuck that, I don't care, says Chris, and her thin arms wrap around me. Even though it's warm she's wearing the same enormously long winter scarf that her head sinks right into. The scarf is now torn in a few places and dull-looking. Still, I can't believe she has held on to this scarf through all that she's been through.

We hug each other as if we were a family. As if we were a family and haven't seen each other for decades—as if one of us, or both of us, were at war the whole time. Now we are safe.

I run into another ghost once I go inside the building. It's Rob, the AA Rob from the harm reduction group, the snake-story Rob. He looks the same, like a middle-aged woman.

He says, It's nice to see you here, stranger.

I hate that I've run into him and I roll my eyes and say, Yeah, I've caved in.

He shrugs and I can just hear him saying something, something preachy but well-meaning.

I gotta go. I think I'm in the wrong room, I say.

I'm not in the wrong room but I can't imagine sitting in the same room as him. I know it would be good for me, healthy for my ego and all that, but I can't stand his eager, earnest eyes. I walk away.

I see him again afterwards. He is walking toward me. Stupid guy.

I think of turning away but then I stop. I remember something. I want to tell him Frankie is okay. I suddenly want him to know this. I want the world to know this. I will take out an ad in the newspaper to let the world know.

Cara yells they're leaving now.

I touch Rob on the sleeve, My son, he's doing well.

If it wasn't for my kids I wouldn't be here, he says and nods.

Me too. I'll see you around, I say. Thank you.

He nods again, Thank *you*.

ARCHAEOLOGY

I t's because I'm a first child.

Because my mother had trouble conceiving and the whole family was waiting for me like some kind of a messiah. And when I was born it was even bigger than they thought it would be because I cried and cried and people forgot that this is what happens.

And after I was born, my beloved grandmother went crazy. She had a history of it. The crazy hung in the air, invisible but there, like an afterimage of smoke. It got lost in all the real smoke that came from her room. She would go through two packs of cigarettes a day. Anxiety. Before she was taken away, I imagine her in her room, in a cloud, waiting, with madness in her hair, standing like a proud captain of a sinking ship.

It was also because after she was gone off to the mental ward, I had an accident when I was an infant. The official story is that I fell off the changing table and hit my head and one of my pupils got stuck. It remained bigger than the other. It is this way to this day.

And, as a toddler, I bit other children. Hard, aggressively. I hated them and they hated me. No one played with me. I preferred to play by myself anyway. It was because of that.

Also, because I got sick later. It was something to do with the urinary tract and we didn't talk about it but I had to spend lots of time in the hospital undergoing painful procedures. I knew that because it happened below my waist, I had to be ashamed of my problem. No one wanted to talk about it. And I was warned enough times that I had to comply with this or the mysterious problem would be revealed to the world. I felt like a freak. Unclean. I still don't know what was wrong.

Anyway. It's because of that.

And because when my sister was born she almost died.

And because I read about skinny girls in magazines and decided that I was fat.

It's also because I idolized Jim Morrison. He was a rock star. And so was I. By nature.

It's also because I read *We Children from Bahnhof Zoo*—a memoir of a thirteen-year-old heroin addict—when I was thirteen and I thought her story was beautiful and tragic. (The author finally gets clean after her closest friends overdose and die, and after she gets tired of selling her ass to get a fix. I look her up online and read that her life was a series of relapses. *Is.* She is using right now in Amsterdam.)

It's because I wanted to be a junkie. I wanted to be tragic. With black eyeliner running down my cheeks and fragile wrists and sores and bruises like tiny flowers in every reddish area of my body.

It's because as a child, my mother made me rewrite the word *butterfly* a hundred times until I got all the letters following a straight line, tilting at the right angles but not too slanted, and with enough curve at the loops.

Because my father said it wasn't even worth his time when I couldn't get arithmetic as he sat there with me, explaining my own homework to me for hours.

Because he shouted. And because she shouted. But they also took me to art museums and my father explained what makes a good poem.

It's because I love my parents too much. Because I saw that they're human but I didn't expect them to be. I expected them to be gods.

It's because we moved to a different country when I was a teenager. I spent countless nights, paralyzed with grief, not sleeping, just replaying an imaginary scene of my grandmother left alone in the apartment that used to be ours and was now filled with the ghosts of us as children, maybe still smelling of our toys. I pictured her unfolding and refolding our kid clothes, wondering about our warm bodies that used to live inside them. I lay there in my new bed, in the new country, screaming in my head, trying to deafen the other sound in my head—of my grandmother shuffling back and forth between the rooms.

It's because of the cocker spaniel, my first dog, that we left behind with my grandmother, that ran up to the elevator door as we were leaving with our suitcases for good. The sad, stupid dog yelped so loud I can still replay that crazed yelping if I make the memory stick long enough.

I never do make them stick long enough.

I probably drank because I could no longer make them stick or because they stuck and I got stuck.

Because I got raped. Or because I didn't really care that I did since by that time things stopped sticking.

And also because I finally felt normal when I drank. Whatever normal was. But unlike many people I was always preoccupied with finding it.

Because I fell in love when I went back to visit the old country and because I had to leave my love. Leave again.

Because the education system failed me. I was the girl who fell through the cracks. I had student loans the size of a small continent. The more loans I had, the more I drank.

Also: the more I drank, the more in love I was. There were many relationships. All of them because. And because of all of them. Especially the last one. This one. With my boyfriend. Because of him. Because I found out he had cheated with the determined lady when I was away in Montreal. Because of that. Because he owned up to it. Because his honesty and his love and care made me feel like I was suffocating.

That too.

Because I can be petty and resentful. I couldn't understand how a woman could do that to another woman, especially one who just had a baby. I obsessed over this. Because of my obsessiveness. My rage.

So that too.

Because I am selfish, unable to see beyond my own wants. The urgency to soothe my internal conflicts, pain, is stronger than my accountability.

Because I got sober and I missed being drunk. I missed it the way I missed everything: with complete abandon.

And because an old lover contacted me, an old crush, really, who wanted to know if I was *me* still. He wrote he missed it so much, the old me. By then I missed me and he just happened to be there at the right moment, I mean his email was. We used to drink together. I read his old email, and all those feelings came back. I wanted to be that old me.

And because there was my best friend's bachelorette and because I asked for a soda and the bartender said—as they always do—*Just* soda? and just like that I changed my mind. No, *vodka* and soda.

And also because I got pregnant.

Because my mother couldn't handle it when I did. She didn't want me to have a baby because it was wrong to have it with this man, in this country, it was the wrong baby.

Her own mother, my beloved grandma, was dying. It drove my mother crazy with worry and guilt. She desperately wanted to go back to the old country. But the would-be baby seemed to be a confirmation that we were staying here for good.

Sometimes, I would pick up the phone wanting to ask my mother: Was it like this for you when you were pregnant? Did you feel like this? What did you do when? What happens after?

Then I would put the phone down. I couldn't call. I remembered. I was told not to call. It was because of that.

Because my mother didn't quite succeed in poisoning me with her own guilt. But I felt poisoned regardless. I felt toxic with rage.

Because I held it together and told myself I will hold it together until I give birth to this child and then I will murder every single perpetrator, starting with myself.

Because of Frankie. Because I couldn't handle all the love.

———

This is the archaeological dig of my addiction.

It's what I think about as we drive along the same gray highways that we did on the way to rehab. This time, however, we're on the way to a hotel where we will stay for a few days as a family, the three of us, just for fun. Frankie is in the back in his car seat asleep. It's Christmas.

We talk about my drinking.

I don't think the *why* is important. I say this as softly as I can.

I know that my boyfriend has every right to ask me about the whys. In his world it has to be sorted, figured out—then you can move on.

Why?

I don't list my explanations. He knows a lot of these explanations already. He has lived through a lot of them with me. I could list them again but I don't believe that any of them are truly, fully the reason why.

This is not an episode of *Intervention*. Life isn't like that. There's no one event, no line that I crossed that I can pinpoint, that has made me an addict. I was always floating and the gravity was pulling me down and then I touched the soft spot in my life and fell right through. And then it happened again. And again.

I try to be gentle with my boyfriend when he asks these questions—why, why, why—but I can't lie to him about the whys. I'm scared to answer, scared to disappoint him with my answer.

I don't know why, I say.

But it's an interesting thing to think about, he says.

It is.

———

I know, I could just lie. Just tell him it was one of those things. Give him that relief. Say it was the shameful medical procedures, the email from the crush, the stress during pregnancy. Anything.

It was anything, really.

CHRIS

It's been seven months since I got sober. I meet with Chris for a coffee. We talk. We talk about lying to each other. I tell her about waiting for her in front of the liquor store that day we took photos. She says she got on the bus and rode the full route before getting off and going to the liquor store in the market where she used to live. She doesn't live there anymore.

She talks about trying heroin for the first time.

Why doesn't she live in the market anymore?

She shrugs. She is homeless now, couch-surfing, staying with her mother when things get really bad.

Today, she's got five days. Again.

Up close I see that her face along the jawline is marred by tiny scabs, scars.

I'm just a fuckup, she keeps saying.

No, you're not.

I am. I don't play music anymore. I never used those pictures because I never made another album. So. I'm a fuckup.

Chris.

It's okay. I'm okay with that.

You've got five days. You're not a fuckup.

Five days. Yay me.

Five days? Do you know how hard it was to get twenty-four hours? Impossible. It was impossible. How do you get five twenty-four hours? I don't know. I don't know how I got to seven months. In a way, my seven months is less than five days.

Maybe, she says.

In sobriety actual time can be—and often is—irrelevant. It is not linear. It stretches, elongating one breath that can last for eternities, and then suddenly contracts, squeezing eternities into one sober breath. Five days is longer than five years for an addict.

Not maybe.

Chris says, Not maybe then. Yeah, you're on to something, for sure. Time is funny in general when you're using. You start okay. You can be okay for a long time. And then the more you do, the worse it gets. It never gets better. The deeper you go, the narrower it gets. Everything just speeds up and shit happens all at once. There's less room and more shit piles up on you.

What happened? I say.

Last week, I shot up. And I got arrested for the first time. I've never been arrested before. So the shit keeps piling up, you know, and the end gives you less space to manoeuvre. And I've no idea where else it's going to take me but I know it's not going to be back up, for sure.

I don't interrupt her. It's not like I myself shy away from addict poetry. And I like listening and watching her so animated, and I like talking about recovery.

I haven't been sleeping lately, Chris says. I'm going nuts.

You think you'll sleep tonight?

She says nothing for a long time. I repeat the question.

A large, loud group of students walks in. They line up for coffee behind all the other lined-up people. We're in the teacher's college building. Everyone is studying one theory or another. Big kids with textbooks, all of them.

Chris's glassy eyes don't seem to register all the tumult.

A thought crosses my mind, that she's shutting down right now, in this very instant, because of the lack of sleep and whatever else is going on—a withdrawal—that she's just shutting down right there.

Finally, she says, Thing is, I'm afraid to wake up. Yeah. I'm afraid to wake up. She looks at me, something like surprise in her enormous eyes.

You mean, you're afraid to be awake.

She nods.

And then, naturally, I understand. It's easier not to wake up. The world goes on. But not with you in it. This is why we're here together, on this side of addiction. We'll always understand what it's like to be afraid to wake up.

When we're finished with our coffees, we go to a meeting together.

Before the meeting is over, I hold her hand as we stand in a big circle with other addicts holding each other's hands, and we recite a pledge to help each other out. It's a silly ritual but it gives the illusion that we're in this together, before we go out into the world again, outside of the twelve-step walls. The bones in Chris's hand are tiny, a bird's skeleton.

I hope she makes it.

But she doesn't. Not yet. Maybe not ever. I find out from Cara a few weeks later that Chris goes out, again, and is still out. *Out* is a popular term for addicts who can't quit.

This sounds as if she has escaped.

Which is the opposite of what's going on.

FALLING

Winter is almost over. I'm in a meeting as usual and the windows are open and you can smell the spring: wet cement after the rain.

The speaker is announced. It's a man I've seen around. Seems like a nice guy though we've never talked. But I see people's faces after they talk to him. They look happy.

The man is older, Irish. He speaks with an accent so thick that I find it too hard to understand him at first. I have to listen carefully, let my ears tune in before I can decode the words. This makes me think of when I drunk-talked. When I started drinking heavily in order to be able to talk in the new language after we moved to Canada. When the drink made it seem as if I had the language tamed and manipulated to serve me.

I recall myself in high school, in a car with a boy, somewhere in a cornfield, a farmhouse somewhere beside the cornfield. In the house, a party, also, a case of beer—mine—emptied, and me, finally brave enough to speak in the new language.

Me, so pretty and teenage and sexy, and talking, talking, talking. The boy's unsure eyes. The boy saying something I couldn't quite hear, as if I was underwater and he was above it, on the safe surface. The sudden realization that I couldn't understand him, and that I wasn't really talking either. It was nonsense falling out of my mouth as I tried to put my mouth on his to make myself shut up. And then the boy, turning his face away and calling me words I did understand: you're fucking crazy.

———

Hey, hey, Cara whispers.

Sorry. I roll my eyes.

She shakes her head in exaggerated fashion, stifles laughter. I love you, she mouths.

The room laughs. I don't catch the joke.

I want to ask Cara to repeat it to me but I feel embarrassed that I didn't hear it and I lose my nerve to ask.

I don't know why I'm getting so distracted. I even check my phone, though I should have it turned off. It beeps once when a text comes through. It's my boyfriend.

We had a nice bath, songs and a story and went to bed, the text reads.

I picture the baby's fat soft body giving off heat like a small generator when he sleeps. In my mind's eye I see his room with its tiny yellow nightlight—just enough of a light to draw out my little boy's impossible loveliness. Arms thrown to the sides, eyelids like shells, thick eyelashes, rosebud mouth. He breathes through his mouth. His breath is sweet.

Right now, in this moment, I am happy and I'm okay with it. Just for now. My boys are at home and I have a home. I don't wake up to my own slow death anymore.

As if on cue the speaker says, I am not afraid to live. Right now. I am not afraid to live.

Right now.

The speaker says that he loved to drink. Why wouldn't he? It was like in that song, where falling feels like flying just for a little while?

The room murmurs in appreciation.

I write it down on a piece of paper, Falling feels like flying.

I think that I could tattoo this somewhere. I want to remember it forever. I want it to be etched into me, stay in my skin. I want it to protect me.

But nothing can protect me. From me. Not even me.

He's been sober for nineteen years now, he tells us. And then his story is done and he's done talking. It was a good talk. The room starts to clap.

Cara whispers in my ear that she's got a car and can drive me. I can't wait to get home tonight.

———

Do I stay sober?

Oh, how would I know? I'm still here. But how can I be sure of anything else?

A NOTE AND ACKNOWLEDGEMENTS

Drunk Mom is an imperfect account of the events that occurred from 2009 to 2010 when I relapsed after three and a half years of sobriety. It's an imperfect account because memory is an imperfect process, a process in which you are the writer and the brain is the editor. By the time it's retrieved it's already been concocted into a story that we need to tell ourselves. I've also read somewhere (I can't remember where) that memory is like any other artifact, prone to erosion. In any event, with these limitations, I've tried to record events faithfully but have taken liberties. I've made changes to the chronology and conflated some events in order to tighten the story. This is by no means a published *journal* of my relapse, and for that reason too all the dialogue is an approximation. I've changed all names and some details to protect the identities of some of the people I write about and, in the case of people like my son and boyfriend, whose identities cannot be protected, to at least soften the glare.

This has been a painful story to tell. I wrote it for three reasons. First, because I hope it will help some of those who are struggling with similar issues, and give others a glimpse into what that struggle is like. This is a story of an addiction but also of parenthood, which is in itself a major mind game for which no one is really prepared. Second, but most important, this book is an attempt to make amends to my greatest love, my son, who I hope will one day be able to forgive me for this transgression. Third, it is a form of apology to both my partner and my sister.

I want to thank the following institutions and people for making my sobriety and/or this book a possibility:

Alcoholics Anonymous

Centre for Addiction and Mental Health

New Port Centre

Beyond Belief agnostic group

Chris Bucci—for taking a chance, for reading and working on my manuscript, and for your superb advocacy as my agent

And everyone at Anne McDermid and Associates

Tim Rostron—for being the perfect editor; I'm eternally grateful and extremely lucky to have been able to work with you

Lynn Henry—for believing in this book and for all your support

Kristin Cochrane

Sharon Klein

Shaun Oakey

And everyone at Doubleday Canada

Jeanne Ryckmans

Rachel Dennis

And everyone at HarperCollins Australia

Patrick Nolan—for believing in this book!

Max Reid

Rebecca Lang

And everyone at Penguin Group (USA)

My partner—for everything, but mostly for being a great dad and for not giving up on me

My sister—for all the love and support; you are the only one who has always stood by me, no matter what

My son—for making my life make sense, for the joy and love like no other love

Ann Smith—for her grace

Belinda Smith—for love and support and incredible bravery that has always inspired me

My parents—for taking a really deep breath when I told you about this book and joking we all move to Goa

Melanie Janisse—for all the love and support

Cheryl Brown—for your love and support

Agalz Miszczyńska

Naomi Gaskin

Maggie Keats

Nicole Deane

Joshua Marc

Adam Nicholls

Betty Doherty

Robin Barnett

Dr. Amita Singwi

Darin Meilleur

D. O'Soup

Mary Shriver

Megan Griffith-Greene

Allison Grange, Bunmi Adeoye, Lisa Hannam, Becky Scott, Kristin Kent, and Ally Tripkovic

All of those who trudge the road of happy destiny

Mothers, fathers, and children affected by addiction